The
Office Game

K.V. Scott, PMP

Published by K.V. Scott
Email: K.Scott@kossencommunications.com
Edited by: Nitara Lee Osbourne
Cover Design and Images by: K.V. Scott
Book Design by: Tamara Cribley, The Deliberate Page

Printed by Createspace
Manufactured in the United States of America

The Office Game
Copyright © 2019 by K.V. Scott

Note: The information presented in this book is for professional, personal, and self-development purposes only. The author is not providing professional career coaching or counseling; the author is not providing legal counsel, accounting, financial, or tax advice; the author is not acting as a therapist, psychologist, or any mental health physician on the reader's behalf. The reader should consult a professional coach, licensed attorney, certified accountant, financial advisor, or tax specialist, licensed therapist, psychologist, or physician if the need for such services arise. The author is not liable for how readers may choose to use this information.

Scott, K.V.
The Office Game

First Printing 2019.
ISBN: 978-0-578-46319-3

Contents

For Ryan, and everyone else in the pursuit of building their professional career.

Introduction

Some people think that talent and hard work are all that is needed to succeed in Corporate America, or the workplace in general. This idealistic fantasy is often portrayed in movies, television shows, and personal testimonials from A-list celebrities and CEOs that have made it or reached the pinnacle of their field.

Year after year, college students from all over the country clamor to get the best internships with the biggest Fortune 500 companies in order to get a competitive advantage before entering the workforce after graduation. Some students are already fast-tracked into a great job because of their family or fraternity/sorority affiliations. However, the vast majority of them will have blazed their own trail to venture into the unknown world of Corporate America without a map. Even the people who have the "golden tickets," often show up to the game without the playbook. Although they seemingly have free admission to opportunity, they still have the same challenges and suffer the same pitfalls.

If they are fortunate enough to land a career positon into today's job market, this is only the beginning. Entry-level and mid-level employees work countless hours of overtime and take on every additional work request, regardless of how difficult or unprofitable. They do this to prove they can go above and beyond what is required, and therefore should be considered for promotions. They are exploited by corporate gate-keepers and have carrots waved in front of them that they will never be able to eat. Each time they are about to reach the metaphorical orange vegetables, or their "time has come," the rules have changed or the focus has shifted; they have to start at ground zero. Oftentimes, people get discouraged or fed up, and decide to leave the company only to find themselves in the same cycle elsewhere.

Some people think they have it figured out with the old adage, "it's not what you know; it's who you know." They see the boss's son get hired to run the division he's unqualified for and his best friend gets hired as a senior executive. They think that they can bypass working hard altogether and opt for the schmoozer that partners with the right manager or director to carry them to the promised land of money, status, and security. Who they know may get their foot in the door, but these types of people are only successful for the moment. This strategy is usually short-lived based on circumstances of the ever-changing corporate environment with management, organizational structures, and most importantly, the perception of their professional brand.

Johnny X was a business professional that started his first job in Corporate America almost 20 years ago. Over the past two decades, he worked in many industries in the communications field—including the financial, non-profit, education, government, technology, sports, insurance, fast-food, hotel, and television. Although the industries and their challenges were extremely different, some basic behaviors and philosophies were the same. He realized that "making it" in Corporate America took more than talent, education, and even knowing the right people.

To really win in the workplace and be the most successful professional that he could be, he knew that he needed to use all of these components to a certain degree, but most importantly, he knew that he needed to know the game and how to play it. "You've got to know how to play the game to make it," is what office veterans, mentors, and even janitors have proclaimed.

Johnny X was exposed to situations like being laid off for a less qualified worker to take his place for lesser pay, being passed over for a promotion was not unheard of, or having his idea stolen by a colleague and passed off as their own was part of the corporate experience.

The funny thing is, no one ever explicitly says what "the game" is. It just seems like that phrase has always been apropos to say when a mistake is made or when something unfair happens in the office.

The Office Game is not about deceiving people or portraying yourself to be something you're not. It's about understanding your environment, knowing how to conduct yourself in certain situations, and how to overcome certain obstacles in your journey throughout your career. It's about applying best practices that professionals before you, have won and lost jobs in order to learn.

It's like the game of basketball. Some teams win by shooting a lot of 3-pointers with small, quick guards, while other teams draft huge 7-foot power forwards to pound the ball in the paint. Both can be equally effective, but it's about your opposition and what works for you that makes the difference.

It was once thought that the saying "you've got to know how to play the game" was a cliché used by people who felt like there was an inside secret to how to do things. When a person suffered a traumatic pitfall at the hands of another colleague or their own doing, there was always someone to remind them that the game had to be played the right way. That phrase was often met with sarcasm and the "now you tell me" look.

It seems that these jewels are typically dropped after the fact. Realizations are met over a drink during happy hour or on the ride home when you replay chains of events back in your head that led to your professional demise.

Taking losses early on in your career will happen, but what if you're able to overcome certain issues early on? What if someone put you *in* the game early enough to beat the curve? For the first time ever, the basic rules of the game are in a book.

This book will give you a basic understanding of how office politics work, how creating your image and brand affects your career, and scenarios of when and where to apply these rules and best practices.

Many say that there is no such thing as "office politics." It's usually the people that either benefit from it, or have never fell victim to it. We also know that everyone's professional experience isn't the same. Every industry has its own rules. People from different demographics have a certain uniqueness to their career experiences.

If you're young, old, female, gay, or physically impaired, you are sure to have particular nuances unique to you. However, there are some universal rules, experiences, and pitfalls that everyone should be prepared for.

The internships and training programs teach you about the company, the job, and about the industry. What they don't always teach you about is one of the most important elements: the people.

Let's not be totally cynical; there are some great people that you will meet throughout your career. There will be some awesome managers, colleagues, mentors, teachers, and best friends that you will come across. On the other hand, there are some people that are power-hungry, ladder-climbers, brown-nosers, leeches, backstabbers, phony, negative thinkers, complainers, and bullies that see you as nothing more than a pawn in *their* way to the top.

What's important to remember is that whether you think you're playing or not, you have to understand that the game will find you. People and situations will remind you that you're playing. You are not watching the game from the sidelines. You are at the line of scrimmage with no referees. There are no out of bounds.

You must be able to determine the game you're playing, know who's on your team, and know when to play offense or defense. More importantly, you want to learn and know how to win. Get some Office Game!

*** GAME TIP ***

Know when to play and when not to. Whether you realize it or not, you're always in the game, but you don't always necessarily have to make a move. Always be observant, but not pressed to always react. It's a chess game, not checkers.

Playbook Notes

CHAPTER 1

TRY-OUTS

Pre-Game Analysis:

    ✗ Lessons from a veteran in the game.

    ✗ Get a glimpse of the dark side of the workplace.

    ✗ The realization that you have a lot to learn.

*The stories told in this book are true, but company and employee names have been changed to protect the privacy and reputations of the entities and individuals involved.

A Story from a Veteran in the Game

About 20 years ago, I started out as a blue-collar laborer loading boxes into 18-wheelers for four hours a day in a warehouse. It was back-breaking work, but it was a very convenient job to have while I was in college. Upon my graduation, my supervisor informed me about a position that was available in the corporate office that was in my marketing field. He told me that he would write me a recommendation letter.

I was the class clown of the bunch who always had people laughing, and I never even considered being promoted as an option. Usually when people went to HR, they were being written up or fired. I couldn't imagine working in those offices every day—until I started the interview process. Everyone was dressed nicely and the administrative assistants brought in donuts each day. I *loved* donuts!

I started to see what was possible. I would have my own desk, telephone extension, computer, and a parking spot in the front of the building. I was thinking that I could get used to this. I was always a great talker, so after a few interviews, I had the General Manager convinced that I was the right person for the job. I got offered the position that same afternoon that I had interviewed. Here I would make my first big mistake. I was so happy to have been hired, I forgot to ask how much I was getting paid. I even came into the office to sign the offer letter and never once asked for more money.

This was lesson number one.

Never accept the initial offer. Always negotiate your salary. This is one of the best times to get yourself a raise. Merit increases don't compare to what you can get on the front end.

Nevertheless, I gladly traded in my denim jeans and work boots for khakis and a button down shirt and tie, even though I only owned two ties at the time. Many of my co-workers from the previous division where I started out a year prior hailed me as the hero that made it out of the fields as a worker bee; I was promoted to a job in the "big house" in Corporate. They treated me like the favorite son that would return to the docks bearing gifts and benefits for everyone. After all, I knew firsthand the plight of the hard working guys in the loading docks, and I was in a position to meet with the HR Manager and the General Manager to talk about their issues. Admittedly, that was the least of my concerns.

I felt like Julia Roberts in *Pretty Woman* trying to adjust to high society.[1] I subconsciously was trying to put the blue-collar life behind me. It wasn't about being a voice for the warehouse anymore. It was about *me*. I was learning how to properly send emails, use Power Point, and run conference calls. I was working with vendors and attending luncheons with senior managers and local luminaries. I loved what I was doing and wanted more of it. I wanted to sit in the big chair at the head of the table. I wanted to make decisions. I wanted to drive the 500S Class Mercedes like my GM.

I learned so much in my first year. I earned a new-found respect from other managers, and I was able to see the reality of what it took to run a company. I learned how our company really made its money, how the organization structure worked, and how to use the tools and resources at my disposal. I learned about the personnel side of our business. I was taught about payroll, the hiring process, how managers disciplined poor performing employees, and how they promoted the good ones. I began to understand why things were the way they were on the front lines, but what was worse was that I was becoming one of them.

It was like the movie *Fast and the Furious* when Brian went undercover and joined Dom's street-racing crew/crime syndicate. Once immersed in the street-racing culture, he became less of a cop and more of a member of the crew.[2]

By the way, if you haven't noticed already, I have a deep love for movies, and reference them often when illustrating points.

Anyway, I felt like I was a corporate guy at this juncture. I still hung out with my warehouse buddies from time to time, but I was never available to really go down there. I always had a meeting, a project, or an event to attend. After a while, my friends/former colleagues began to notice. When I went into the main break room, I started feeling like Alonzo from the movie *Training Day* when the hood turned on him. I was losing the genuine love of my people and I was now only being tolerated.

I also got my first glimpse of the dark side of Corporate America. I saw the way my reputation could affect my future in terms of getting promoted, laid off, or worse. I saw people being manipulated and naïve people being exploited out of their ideas and work that they had done. I would sit in a meeting and listen to a person deliver a great presentation filled with great ideas and promise. They would shake hands with the management team and then leave the conference room. Five minutes after they were gone, the management team would start their roasting session. They picked apart every detail of what that person had just presented. I heard personal issues and complaints about people, I heard revenge plots, and I listened to people make mockeries of other people's career aspirations. I had my first real glimpse behind the curtain and it was terrible.

The institution of Corporate America as I knew it would be forever tainted. I recalled back in my early warehouse days hearing old woe-is-me stories and conspiracy theories from older employees. They talked about how they were screwed over by management for promotions or how they were suspended over a personal dispute that bled over into work, and so on. I knew at this point that these instances were not just paranoid conspiracy theories. Some of these stories and assumptions were true. I began to think about myself. If so much was openly shared about other people, what was being said about me? Who was plotting to take my spot? Who could I really trust?

As I witnessed more of these situations, I began to wonder what went wrong with this person and that person during their tenure. How did they arrive at this crossroad? What actions or circumstances set off this chain of events? I started piecing facts together and going back in history, replaying moments in my head. I realized some folks had been set up for failure months ago.

I had a really close friend at work named Tony, but we used to call him "Boney T," which was what Chris Rock's mailroom character's name was in the movie *Boomerang*.[3]

Tony got the name because he was skinny. He was a great worker, but he was very opinionated and had a great influence over the warehouse workers. He was an old head from the Magnolia Projects in Uptown New Orleans. He didn't take any nonsense from anyone. Not even managers. Even though people were intimidated by the street side of him, he was the best at what he did. Boney T was also one of the smartest people I knew. If there was a way to get something done more efficiently, he would figure out how. If there was a policy or new rule coming down from Corporate that he knew wouldn't work, he'd push back. More importantly, he would have the troops pushing back with him. He was like the warehouse combination version of Tupac and Martin Luther King Jr.

Needless to say, Boney T wasn't liked very much by the supervisors because they thought that he was good enough to take their jobs away. However, they found comfort in the fact that he was rough around the edges and would never have "the look" required to be in management. Knowing this, they would always invite him into strategy meetings, kiss his butt just enough to steal his ideas, and pass them off as their own.

After a while, Boney T got hip to what was happening. They were ripping off his ideas for months. Other people were getting credit for implementing his safety concepts and process improvement plans. Some even got awards and promotions. He had even gotten into an argument with one of his supervisors over it. He was written up for cussing on the floor. Boney T decided that he would stop sharing his ideas and being used by these distrustful managers, so he started declining the meeting invites and sharing less. Sadly, it was too late. The management staff exhausted the pilfering of his skills and best practices for so long that there was almost nothing left to take. I heard his Manager say one day in passing to me that they have been able to create 10 workers like Tony on the warehouse floor thanks to his own exploitation. They said that it would be a matter of time before they got rid of him. I asked if we were laying people off because I couldn't understand how they would be able to get rid of a guy who was so valuable to the company. This guy was the real Corporate MVP!

The Manager told me at my desk that they had been working on getting rid of him for a year. They were accumulating information on him via emails, small write-ups, and through casual conversations. In a vulnerable moment at the office happy hour at a local bar, Boney T slipped up and told the manager, who he had been cool with, that he started smoking marijuana to deal with his back issues.

Our Company had a strict drug policy and the Manager was going to set Boney T up to be "randomly" tested. I asked the Manager why he would do something like that.

He just shrugged it off and said, "Because he's too arrogant. Plus, we know all of his tricks, and now we don't have to put up with him."

I thought to myself, wow, this is like a mafia hit. I marveled at how carefree and almost downright ecstatic he was about what they were going to do. I had to cut the conversation short because I had a meeting to get to.

As I sat in my status meeting, I began to feel conflicted because Boney T was my buddy. I couldn't let him be set up for the "okey-doke," but I was afraid to break rank. If they were coming after Boney T, surely they would come after me. Did I really want to get involved to that extent?

After a few hours of my personal deliberation, I decided to take Boney T to lunch. I was always a very talkative person, but that day I was struggling with my words. I tried to figure out a way to tell Bony T what was about to happen to him. I attempted to tell this long, drawn-out parable, but he knew me too well for that.

He was sitting across from me waiting for me to spit out the juicy information I had. "You always got to act like it's story time," he joked. It made me laugh, and I immediately felt comfortable to share. I just came out with it.

"Man, they are gunning for you to get you out of here. They are trying to set you up with a drug test," I blurted out. Before I could continue, I was interrupted by Boney T's laughter. Once he let out a loud sigh, I continued, "Man, I 'm serious. "You're about to get fired. They've been milking you for all of your skills."

Suddenly Boney T stopped laughing, and a very serious look came upon his face. He took a couple of sips from his Burger King cup, leaned in, and started talking in a whisper, but a strong tone. "Look here, youngster, you don't think I know that? They been trying to let me go for 10 years, but they can't. You know why? They need me and I make sure of it." He took a few bites of his burger, a few more sips of his drink, and started talking again.

"Youngster, you got to know how this game works, man. Never show all your cards—ever! I know they steal some of my ideas. Well, at least the ones I put out there. The bigger and more important ones I keep for myself. They get what I want them to have. Sometimes you lose a little now to win later."

I was listening intently, but I was thinking, "What about the drug test? You're still a weed head."

Before I could say it out loud, he said, "I drink brown liquor and I've been smoking cigarettes since the 1980s. I haven't smoked weed since I was in my 20s, youngster, but I know they smoke weed, so I talk about it with them so they can think we have some type of connection."

He went on for about 20 minutes on all the ways he had managed to win the chess match between him and management. He talked about his 401(k), his retirement plans, and the benefits of working in the warehouse for all those years. I even found out that he had his own tax business that he ran on the side and that it made more money than his day job. I soaked it all up like a sponge. It was like Moses coming down from Mount Sinai and giving the children of Israel the Ten Commandments. He gave me valuable information from an employee's perspective on career management and how important it was to protect myself. I totally underestimated him, which was another lesson I learned. We went back to work that day and everything was back to normal. They were never able to fire Boney T and he continued to do his work.

After that day, all that I could think about was our conversation. I coupled what Boney T shared and my experiences working in HR and I began to think.

What would happen if they came for me? What would I do to make myself more valuable? How would I protect, improve, and preserve my image amongst my colleagues and senior management team?

I didn't have all of the answers, but this was a great foundation to start with.

Post-Game Takeaways:

✗ Learn from my Corporate America experience with transitioning from a laborer in the warehouse to working in the company's office. This included changing my mindset and learning to observe how things were done in order to both protect and elevate myself.

✗ Learn from Boney T's experience of playing the office game. He understood how to play the game of politics by connecting with and giving upper management just enough to keep himself valuable to the company, but kept his really brilliant ideas for himself. He took initiative and created a side business, which allowed him to not be completely dependent on his job.

✗ Understand that there is a "dark side" to the workplace and learn how to maneuver your way through it.

✗ Continue to learn from your own experiences.

*** GAME TIP ***

Learn as much as you can about the culture of a company before you get there. For example, you can find out information online via social media, former employees, and news stories (scandals, CEO changes, earnings announcements, and so on). Also, learn where the company is within its lifecycle to determine whether they are in the launch, growth, downsizing, or maintaining phase. This should be enough for you to decide if you want to join the company or not.

Playbook Notes

CHAPTER 2

FIRST IMPRESSIONS

Pre-Game Analysis:

✗ Tips for making a first impression in the office.

✗ Protect your personal business/information.

✗ Lay the foundation for your brand.

"You never get a second chance to make a first impression," the old saying goes. This rings true when you are starting a new job. From the time you enter the doors, you are being judged and sized up by everyone that sees you. They analyze everything from what you're wearing, the way you're walking, your hairstyle, your facial expressions, the employees you already know, and even down to the type of backpack or briefcase you're carrying. People are figuring out if they should fear you or to take you under their wings.

In most cases, when a person is starting a new job, they arrive at the office enthusiastic and unaware of what's going on. They are just happy to be there and thrilled about their new position.

Nevertheless, in your moment of excitement, veteran employees have already begun chattering about you, they have decided if you're stuck up, naïve, a nerd, or if you're there to potentially take their place. Some have even begun working on your demise.

It's sort of like the stories that we hear about when someone enters prison for the first time. The inmate's first walk-through projects the initial image of that person. Fellow inmates begin making decisions on whether to respect or to exploit the new convict. There are usually three types of people that enter the prison. There's the experienced career criminal with his 24-inch guns, tattoo-covered body, a slow walk, his head up, and fists clutched. Then there's the guy who is terrified and afraid of his own shadow. His eyes are riddled with fear as he scans the entire room in sheer horror. Lastly, there's everyone else in the middle who makes up the majority. The challenge with this group is making sure they project the right image to make their experience as comfortable as possible.

This same psychology is present in the workplace. Although your physical safety isn't on the line, your career, reputation, and livelihood can be. The general rule of thumb is to be yourself, but rather a conservative version. Not too far left or right, but somewhere in the middle. Use the Denzel Washington meter.

Malcolm from *Malcolm X* is too far right.[4]

Alonzo from *Training Day* is too far left.

John Q from the movie by the same name is where you want to be.[5]

Please note that there are also "secret agents" in the workplace that are going to do some reconnaissance work on you as soon as they find out your full name. Be prepared that these operatives (colleagues) will google your name and search for all of your social media pages to be able to give the 4-1-1 to your other co-workers. It is strongly advised that once you are hired, that you move your Facebook page to private if it's not set there already. Delete any Instagram photos or posts that you feel may be an issue or come back to bite you. The current climate of sensitivity is at an all-time high and you don't want to be labeled before you even get through the door to present yourself. Everything on the internet about you is fair game. Once you enter the company, there are no out of bounds. It's go time.

Tips to Make a Great First Impression

Dress for work. The first step is shaping your image from top to bottom. What you project makes a difference, so you will need to do a little recon work yourself. Ask your hiring manager or boss what the dress code is. Search their website for activities and pictures of employees. Do a drive-by visit to find out what they are wearing.

In this new age, we have gotten away from the traditional mode of dress. From the first time I started working in Corporate America, I knew I had to dress the part. I went to Macy's and bought the corporate nerd starter kit wardrobe for the office. I bought a pair of black, blue, and khaki pants; two white, one powder blue, and a black button down shirt; four assorted color polos; and a pair of brown walking shoes.

All I knew is what I saw on TV and the movies. I remember that I watched the film *Mo' Money* back in 1992 where John Stewart (Damon Wayans) got a job at the Dynasty Card company office. He went from being a street hustling con-man to an entry-level credit card processor. His first move in this new role was to dress up enough to assimilate into the new corporate environment he was thrusted into.[6]

I was not green to how Wall Street stock brokers and D.C. politicians dressed with their three-piece Armani suits and the like, but I always knew that high-end dressing was for the big wigs and upper management. At the time, I knew that I at least had to be John Stewart.

In the present-day working environment, the dress code has become increasingly relaxed. Back in the 1990s when I was a stock clerk at a local Walgreens Pharmacy, we had to wear a button-down shirt and tie with the green Walgreens vest. Today, those same stock clerks are wearing T-shirts with the "Hello, My name is…" sticker on the front.

When Johnny X moved from the D.C. area to Atlanta, Georgia, he worked in an insurance office where everyone wore polo shirts and jeans just about every day. The women wore open-toed shoes and the guys wore full beards and Air Jordan basketball sneakers. This was not the white shirt and tie standard that he was used to in the nation's capital. The more he traveled and talked with people, he realized dressing up wasn't as important anymore, so he conformed as well. After all, he had some Marvel T-shirts he wanted to wear anyway.

Then something amazing happened. Johnny X noticed a guy named Jimmy who dressed the way he used to dress back in his D.C. days at the PR firm. Jimmy came to work each day with a pair of slacks and a dress shirt. A few days out of the week he would even wear a bow-tie. Johnny X teased him about having a very expensive dry cleaning bill, but Jimmy just laughed it off and would jokingly reply back that he was comfortable.

What Johnny X didn't know was that Jimmy stood out to management. Not only was he dressed sharply, but he looked more professional to management and they became interested in what type of work he did. Their senior manager remembered that Jimmy wore the bow-ties all of the time when he came to visit the site. Naturally, when Jimmy interviewed for a supervisor's position, he stood out in the manager's mind. Eventually, he went on to get the job.

Jimmy ran into Johnny X in the breakroom and Jimmy told him that he had been promoted. Johnny X congratulated him, but still teased him about using his wardrobe to kiss up to management. Jimmy laughed it off, but before leaving the breakroom he turned serious for a moment and whispered in a deep mumble to Johnny X, "Sometimes you have to dress for the job you want, not the job you're in."

The rule of thumb is to dress one step higher than your co-workers. You can still enjoy the freedoms of having a relaxed dress code, but always bear in mind that it is the first line of your image. It can work for or against you. Make sure you dress-it-up for meetings, when you'll be with clients, or when you're in the community.

There is a science to the unspoken dress code at large. Mondays are the days you should wear your best outfits. People are focused on the first day of the week. As the week wanes on, if there are no senior or client meetings, you can put aside the button down shirt for a polo.

You should also consider dressing down at least one day of the week, and the preferred day is casual Friday. You want to be able to show people the contrast and that you can fit in. Some try to maintain the Saks 5th Avenue look all week, and in most cases, come across as trying too hard. It's good to strike a balance. You have to be careful. If you're a guy, please don't wear skinny jeans. If you're a woman, please don't wear your Friday night clubbing outfit.

Be smart, but not a know-it-all. Most people hate a know-it-all, especially one that shows up and proves to be one out of the gate. Employees are automatically territorial towards a new employee and don't feel like they have earned the right to correct people or insert their opinion so quickly.

There is a healthy balance to this. If someone asks you for help, feel good about helping them and showing off your expertise. However, if you overhear a conversation that you are dying to interject into, exercise some restraint and just put the topic into your mental rolodex for later. You have to be patient and sit in the cut. Just observe how it plays out, see who answers the question, or who saves the day. Notice how your colleagues respond to that person. In most cases, these topics will come up again, and you will have a better perspective on the culture and who the key players in the office are. This will be valuable to you down the road when it comes to establishing yourself as the alpha-employee. In the meantime, your job is to listen. Let everyone show their hands, while you learn as much as you can about them. Let people underestimate you if they like.

People typically form preconceived opinions and they have a natural tendency to underestimate others. According to *The 48 Laws of Power* by Robert Greene, the 19th Law of Power states that you should "Know who you're dealing with—do not offend the wrong person."[7]

When people don't know who you really are and assume they are superior to you, this serves as a huge advantage. It's like guarding a short person in basketball. You assume that he doesn't have jumping abilities until he does a backdoor cut and dunks on you. Ease in, grasshopper.

The type of image you want to build within those few moments of initial conversations is that you are at the very least polite, intelligent, and assertive when necessary. What you say will not only have value, but will be greatly appreciated. As time goes on, you will never have to aggressively assert yourself because people will just come to you organically. You will then be a valuable resource with a large cache of intellectual currency and power. You can become the Confucius of the workplace.

Professional past. Although people are going to google you and scour your LinkedIn profile anyway, don't spend a lot of time talking about where you used to work. People are really judgmental when it comes to your previous place of employment. It's like being in a previous relationship with someone and you are always bringing up your ex. It's okay to say where you worked if someone asks. It's also okay to draw from previous experience. You just shouldn't use it to try to elevate yourself from your new co-workers. It can become annoying after a while.

Let's take a look at an example. Johnny X started a new project manager position at a small tech firm. Every time there was an issue, he began his feedback with, "At Microsoft..."

Some employees appreciated his past experience with the large Fortune 500 Company, while most scoffed at him under their breath thinking, "then why don't you still work there?" or "if he says that one more time..." They got the picture. He used to work for Microsoft, but it sounded like he needed to name drop it all of the time to make people listen to his point.

You don't want to be the person that brags about their former life with their professional Hollywood mate to their new partner and friends who are living the simple life. Instead, preface your statements with, "what I have done in the past is..." or "I have seen it done like this before."

Personal life. People often become close to the people that they work with. Spouses and best friends sometimes meet in the office. However, these relationships develop organically over time and there are mixed results on whether or not they end with happy endings. Always err on the side of caution when it comes to exposing personal details about yourself.

Your personal life is important to keep private as possible as a new employee, and sometimes even as a seasoned employee. There should be a distinct line between your professional and personal life as you are starting out. Today's transient work environment and rigorous schedule grouped with the blurred line of business socializing, make this task very difficult.

In the entertainment and sports industry, athletes and actors/actresses alike have leveraged their personal lives to enhance their brand. Many athletes have successfully been able to integrate their spouses and children into the spotlight, which has resulted in more endorsements for them and their families. Additionally, their brands have been enhanced with universal family appeal.

Nevertheless, you are most likely not a superstar on the world stage. You don't want to compromise your career and your opportunities based on personal opinions of others who are either your competition or people in power.

It's recommended that you make the necessary adjustments to your social media pages by making your profiles private, deleting your political posts from the web, and removing any provocative photos. The challenge in taking these steps is that people who don't know who you are will look you up and fill in the blanks on what they *think* you are about. The other option is to make sure you have a professional online presence.

Some say that you should not care about what people think about you. In your social circle, perhaps this advice will serve you well. However, in the office, you should absolutely care about what people think. Your reputation is vital in this environment. People who prove to be trustworthy over time, and through interaction of mutual disclosure, can begin to filter into your personal life.

It's really easy to fall victim in this space because people want to fit in. Some people can make you comfortable when they are really just pumping you for information to size you up or to use at a later date. Just like in life, once people find out what's important to you, they can use it to their advantage. When they have access, they have an advantage that can be used against you for the duration of your employment with your current company. They also can misinterpret and misrepresent your social media postings and paint you in a really bad light.

People are idealistic and believe that their co-workers that are in positions of power are always going to operate with the strictest level of integrity when it comes to workplace matters. Most believe that employers don't show favoritism or bias toward certain staff members. That is a flat out lie. The misconception is perpetuated throughout Corporate America and reinforced by the fact that it's ethically wrong, and in some cases, even protected by laws.

Think about it: when a person goes to college, they may join a sorority or fraternity, honor society, or club. Additionally, as professionals, people join trade associations, unions, and religious and social organizations. Often times, people will leverage these affiliations in the job market. How many people do you know have a job because their fraternity brother pulled a few strings for them? Or what's worse, when people have been denied *because* of their affiliations. Although it's discrimination on the surface, employers will never admit that they didn't promote a person because they were part of the rival sorority.

Let's discuss a specific instance. A Michigan graduate started a new job. The first day he came in, he placed a huge Michigan flag in his cubical. He wore his Wolverine sweatshirt on casual Friday and talked trash to anyone who listened. Meanwhile, he didn't realize that his manager graduated from Ohio State University. When it was time to choose the next manager, he was equally matched with another candidate, and his boss had to decide with his gut. Guess what, the Wolverine-sweatshirt-wearing employee lost out.

If you are going to share things, it is best to do so organically once you have had an opportunity to establish a good professional reputation for yourself. Do note that there are facts about you that you won't be able to keep to yourself, but you do control the amount of detail you share about them.

Post-Game Takeaways:

✗ Be polite, respectful, and listen.

✗ First impressions, image, and what others think of you matters.

✗ Keep in mind your tips to make a great first impression in the workplace:
1. Dress for work.
2. Be smart, but not a know-it-all.
3. Professional past. (Don't name-drop your previous employer.)
4. Personal life. (Be cautious as to how much of yourself you share before your co- workers even get a chance to know you in person.)

*** GAME TIP ***

Ask the hiring manager what the dress code is, and when possible, take a look around the office during your interview process and dress one step above it. For men, it's a good idea to keep a white button down shirt in the car just in case; for women, having a white blouse and closed-toe shoes on deck will always have you prepared to be dressed appropriately for any situation.

*** GAME TIP ***

When you can help it, wait about two weeks before you let people know anything personal about you. Be a positive, fun, and professional person, but be a mystery. You want your reputation built on your skills, attitude, and ability to connect with people. You don't want people to have a preconceived thought about who you are based on your affiliation with an organization or their perceived beliefs.

Playbook Notes

_____

_____

_____

_____

_____

_____

_____

_____

_____

_____

_____

_____

_____

_____

_____

_____

_____

_____

_____

_____

_____

_____

_____

_____

_____

_____

_____

_____

_____

_____

_____

_____

_____

_____

_____

_____

_____

_____

_____

_____

CHAPTER 3

GETTING SETTLED

Pre-Game Analysis:

- ✗ Set up your workspace.

- ✗ Learn about your location.

- ✗ Be a great teammate; share a desk.

- ✗ Be a reliable office resource.

Set up your Desk for Home Field Advantage

You have now officially started your new job. You have made it through the barrage of awkward first impressions with the employees who were there to genuinely meet you or size you up. Hopefully, you have successfully projected your desired image to your manager and whomever you came into contact with. You now have a place to sit, which will now be known as your home away from home.

Some say how you keep your desk is how you keep your home. People get the premise, but it's not a universal rule. The two places are completely different. The biggest difference is that home has no boundaries and some offices have strict rules in their code of conduct policies about how to maintain your desk.

However, unlike your man cave at home, or your "she shed," you want to make sure you don't give people too much information about you before you meet. Don't divulge any details about yourself and what you're interested in with the materials, pictures, and coffee mugs at your desk. Build a foundation by them meeting you first, then knowing your interests. Sometimes people will make an immediate assumption about you just because of what they see at your desk.

Johnny X worked for an IT company. He sat next to a Software Engineer named Ralph who was a sloth that had just started with the company. Ralph was a 40-year-old overweight, bald guy, who wore the same dirty pair of khakis several days in a row with a dingy MIT sweatshirt. He loved Milky Ways and seemed to be allergic to throwing them away too. He had Cleveland sports teams' paraphernalia all over his area, which was also terrible in itself.

Needless to say, Ralph's desk was filthy and his seat smelled like boiled bologna. After about a week of complaints, his manager came by and told him that he had to clean his space and maintain it. We couldn't do anything about the dirty pants, but the pod had a standard of cleanliness. The team was always on him about keeping his space clean. Johnny X even bought some air fresheners to plug in at his desk to block the smell.

The unfortunate part is that Ralph was a borderline genius and could solve almost any technical issue, but people only viewed him as the stinky guy in the pod, or "Big Cheese" as he was called behind his back. Johnny X learned that something as basic as how he kept his desk affected his colleagues' opinions of who he was.

There is an art to your work space and the image that you project. When you first arrive on the job and get your desk, people watch to see what you have, because to a keen eye, it will tell them everything that they need to know about you. It tells on your personality, such as whether or not you're organized. It speaks to your values and your vices. Out of curiosity, people want to know your business as much as possible. More importantly, they want to know what your weaknesses are and what to use to their advantage.

What's the lesson here? Don't tip your hand too early to your new office mates. Don't let them know who your favorite sports team is or how many vacations that you have taken. If you're an Ohio State fan and your boss is a Michigan fan, you may be in trouble. Many relationships have started off on the wrong foot because of sports, fraternity/sorority affiliations, or school rivalry situations.

One of the first tasks to place on your to-do list is to get your office supplies, personal necessities, and snacks that you will need for your desk. Get your staplers, pens, mouse pad, posted notes, coffee mug, tissues, bandages, medicine, gum, and so on. Make sure your snacks are sealed and non-perishable to avoid from drawing any unnecessary odors or critters within your space. Having these items on-hand is good to do for several reasons.

Reasons to be Prepared

Don't be the neighbor that always wants to borrow something. It's like being the neighbor (where you live) that always asks to borrow lawn equipment, sugar, wine openers, or parking spots.

If you are always without the essentials that you need to work, people will view you as irresponsible and unorganized. It doesn't matter how great you are at what you do, people will never fully trust you.

Show them you are resourceful. Be more "Batman," and less "Superman." This means you have the utility belt, which prepares you for any situation; versus being like Superman or Superwoman who rely on super powers to deal with situations as they happen.

When you're stocked, people will think that you are focused/resourceful. Resourceful people are always needed. Most importantly, they are always remembered. When project managers build their teams, they typically recruit the people they know will bring something to the table. Sometimes they may not have ever worked with you at all, but will remember how you helped them out at some point. Before you know it, people will come to you for other work-related needs. They will be curious to know what else you can do. Subconsciously, being prepared draws people to you and reinforces the idea that you are a great person.

Connecting with people early on builds trust. Just as you should do when you move into a new apartment building or subdivision, you need to meet your neighbors. You should know who's sitting around you and what they do. During times of "war" or times of "survival," it will be to your advantage to know this information.

Immediately introduce yourself and add them to your internal IM list. You want to be able to keep tabs on them as easily as possible. Furthermore, you need to know who's sitting around you when you are talking about business-related matters, appropriate-level personal discussions, or simply discussing people. Knowledge is power in the office. You could be sitting five feet away from the enemy who's taking notes from every conversation that you have. Pay attention to the people around you and their movements.

After a few weeks, you should know who's working from home on Fridays, who's always late for work, who's more likely to spill information, and which colleagues hang out together. Make a mental note of the items that they have at their desks. Check to see if they have family photos, team logos, trophies, plants, pictures of pets, or political memorabilia. They may have a specific interest like collecting refrigerator magnets that will be good to know when the time is right.

In "hoteling" situations, master how to effectively share desks. Nowadays, some companies are really cheap and some have adopted a new industry practice called "hoteling." This is when employees do not own their desk, but simply show up and sit at whatever workstation is available. This creates all types of problems for people in the office, especially new employees. Although you're not able to put your own personal touch on your space, now is the time to show them you're a team player.

Determine who has a distinct preference of sitting in a certain area; let them have those seats. You find somewhere close by, but always be flexible to sit anywhere. It's really good to not get attached in these types of office arrangements. Be like water and go with the flow. You don't want to tick off managers and obnoxious creatures of habit who will die if they don't get their seat. Additionally, people will appreciate you holding it down for them if you happen to arrive early enough to do so. Fighting over seats is pretty juvenile and it doesn't make you any friends. Well, most of the time. There are exceptions.

When Johnny X played football back in high school, he was a scrawny freshman that was embarrassed about changing his clothes in front of all of the older players. He was hazed as a freshman every chance that the team got. Nevertheless, there were days when the team played away from school. One of these times, Johnny X thought that it would be a good idea to take the first locker in the row closest to the door. He thought that it would reduce his chances of getting molly-whopped by the team. However, the Quarterback of the team Kyle Mills was basically an arrogant jackass who felt like he should always have the first locker. So after the first game, the offensive lineman jumped on Johnny X, and Mills poured Gatorade all over Johnny X's clothes in the locker room. He told him never to take the first locker again. Johnny X learned quickly that placement matters. Next away game, he just took the second locker.

If you're going to share a desk that other people constantly want, and you don't want to opt out of a certain desk as a courtesy, just be prepared to deal with the consequences by standing your ground at the beginning.

You can still be polite, but firm with a smile. Sometimes it's not worth your health or sanity to take a bad seat. For instance, if the only other seats are next to the bathrooms, or if you prefer the window seats, or if there is an annoying person that you want to get away from. Those are good reasons to sit where you want. In those situations, when you *can* be like flowing water, but you *have* to be like ice, choose sanity over charity.

Know the building you're working in. Knowing where you are *going* is just as important as knowing where you *are*. After your manager or colleague gives you the first-day-elementary-school-field-trip version of an office tour, take an afternoon to roam the halls of the building to learn your way around the place *on your own*. Be proactive. You don't want to just know where you come into the building, but you need to be privy to where the alternate exits are located. Find out where the restrooms are, the best vending machines, and where the smokers go to talk during their daily 47 smoke breaks.

A big one is that you should do your best to learn where the conference rooms are. You will run into a lot of managers and executives when they are looking for the conference room. Not only will this help you look like a person who knows what you are doing, but it provides you some one-on-one time and some visibility with the senior people of your company. At the very least, they will remember that you found the correct conference room and saved them from being late for a meeting. This advice will help you navigate through your "first-day-of-school" type of situations. This gets you settled in your space so that you can begin doing your job, and eventually, building your career.

Know the places and resources around the building. Not only should you know about the building that you're working in, you should learn about important locations around your office. It's always good to have multiple ways to get to work if there is a traffic jam or if there is bad weather. Furthermore, it's good to know where restaurants, gas stations, and where clothing stores are as well. How many times have managers or senior vice presidents come to town and asked where the best places are to have lunch?

Knowing where to get the best seafood or barbecue are great pieces of information to have in your personal database. Never underestimate how important knowing where a great restaurant or Starbucks is. Next to conference rooms, places to eat or where to get catering from are the next most important nuggets of wisdom on the list. Learn who the managers of those places are. Being able to plug the name of the manager to the people you are sending to these places helps—especially if you can get them to offer a discount or compliment you even if you're not there.

This goes back to the idea of having your desk laid out as your own personal command center, being organized, and being well-informed by taking initiative to learn what is necessary. The details of knowing where everything is in the building and notable places around your facility makes you more of a valuable resource. It keeps your name in the mouths of important people that will need your expertise and will value your opinions.

Back in 2012, Johnny X was working for a technology company and the HR Director Terry Wilkes was coming in town to visit for an all employee meeting (AEM). He was interested in having authentic Texas barbecue while visiting, and the majority of the people on Johnny X's team did not know where to go. Everyone was throwing out generic ideas like Chili's, TGI Fridays, and the like.

Johnny X interjected and told Terry that he regularly had lunch at an old mom & pop barbecue rib joint about a mile away from the office. He told him that it was the best barbecue in Austin, Texas and that the family had owned the restaurant for almost 30 years.

The team of 12 people, including Terry, went to have barbecue. When they got there, the waitresses all knew Johnny X. He asked for the best tables in the house because he had brought in a special guest. They provided Johnny X and his party great seats, excellent service, and they even accommodated them with free slices of pecan pie. The manager went over to Johnny X to give him props on how professional he was and how courteous he was to the staff. The manager even witnessed Johnny X working on his laptop while he ate, and he acknowledged this as well. It was a great marketing plug for Johnny X to say the least.

The biggest reward was that Johnny X got an opportunity to talk one-on-one with Terry about his project idea, and of course, it got approved. Terry asked Johnny X to get with his Executive Administrative Assistant to set up a meeting that next week. During the afternoon meeting, Terry gave Johnny X a huge shout-out for recommending the restaurant. Some people wondered how Johnny X ended up going to lunch with Terry.

Some just saw Johnny X in a new light. Terry had stamped him as a "somebody."

For Johnny X, that lunch meeting led to him being able to launch his own internal employee training program that got him promoted later that year. It was all because he knew about the area he worked around. All it took was some preparation and a little barbecue.

Post-Game Takeaways:

✗ Set up your desk by getting organized with the essential items, which includes office supplies, personal necessities, and sealed (non-perishable) snacks.

✗ Be a prepared individual and remind yourself of the reasons that preparation is important:

1. Don't be the neighbor that always wants to borrow something.
2. When you're stocked, people will think that you are focused/resourceful.
3. Connecting with people early on builds trust.
4. In "hoteling" situations, master how to effectively share desks.
5. Know the building you're working in and the places/resources around the building.

*** GAME TIP ***

Whatever mobile device you own, whether it's an iPhone, Android, or any other device, make sure you have a charger at your desk. Not only for yourself, but for a neighbor who may need one as well. It's a great way to earn favor in your space. Saving someone from a dying smartphone is like giving someone a pencil before the SATs. They will be forever in your debt.

Playbook Notes

_____
_____
_____
_____
_____
_____
_____
_____
_____
_____
_____
_____
_____
_____
_____
_____
_____
_____
_____
_____
_____
_____
_____
_____
_____
_____
_____
_____
_____
_____
_____
_____
_____
_____
_____
_____
_____
_____
_____

ALLIANCES AND RELATIONSHIPS

Pre-Game Analysis:

- ✗ What are interpersonal skills?

- ✗ People you need to meet.

- ✗ People you need to watch out for.

- ✗ Categorize people in the office.

The information from this point on is all about the most significant elements of having office game that you will use for the rest of your career. For as long as you have one, you will need to be able to deal with people, while protecting/building your brand and reputation. The core skill set in addition to your job skills is your interpersonal skills. The ability to connect with people and effectively communicate is critical. If you're shy, you'll need to work on coming out of your shell because working through politics, dealing with haters, and collaborating with colleagues will require you to master your own ingenuity to interact productively.

Interpersonal skills are defined as those that are used by a person to interact with others properly.

Must-Have Skills for Professionals in the Workplace

1. Be self-aware.

2. Be able to read and translate nonverbal communication.

3. Be respectful and understanding of others.

4. Be a great communicator.

5. Be an active listener.

A lot of people think that because they have great public personalities, or are charming with the opposite sex, that they have great interpersonal skills. However, what many fail to understand is that although people are people, the office is a different terrain with a different set of rules. It's like college sports is to professional sports. You may think you know how to play the game, but the rules and politics around the game are much different from each other. You can find yourself short-changed or on the outside looking in if you don't know how to move. So when you enter the workplace, make sure that this is something that you work on constantly. It's a skill that takes discipline, honesty, and consistency.

The relationships and alliances that you form throughout the company will be absolutely critical to your success. This includes your ability to deal with enemies and adversity. Issues and politics will ultimately find you and you just want to be ready to deal with them. Remember that *the game is on at all times.* Never assume that you can let your guard down and be your normal self that you would be at home with your buddies or your girlfriends. It doesn't matter if you think you are close with your team. It doesn't matter if your colleagues have shared things with you. You always have to be professional, politically correct, and guarded with your sensitive information at all times. Never surrender to false comfort at a lunch meeting, a happy hour function, a holiday party, or a conference call. Once you let someone behind your "wall," you will never get them back over. This is not to say that you can't be friendly with your colleagues or laugh at a joke in a meeting. The advice here is to not over-share your information.

Types of Data to Keep to Yourself

1. Personal business (marital issues, finances, political/in-depth religious views).

2. Opinions of colleagues and their actions.

3. Your business plans or an idea that you plan to share with the leadership team.

The key to this dynamic is to be friendly and open enough for others to be comfortable enough to share their information with you, without you having to give up your own. You can share material on the surface that they could easily discover with a Google search, but make this superficial level of intelligence appear to be deeper than what it is. Allow them to reveal their deep revelations and reward them with your secrecy.

You then need to do reconnaissance work on everyone you come into contact with, especially your management team. There is a lot of high level surface data that you need to know, such as your co-workers' educational background, technical certifications, and association memberships. The first obvious reason is because you need to know what you're up against. Secondly, you need to know what you have in common with your colleagues to leverage it later in the future. You might have gone to the same university, belong to the same fraternity/sorority, or you might be in the same association. This would be to your advantage at the right time. In addition, there's the dark side of the paradigm. You want to know if they have gone to your rival university. Are they part of the young Republicans Club, but you happen to be a Democrat?

You don't need to go out with a questionnaire and survey all of your colleagues. You can use more covert resources to get the information you need. The days you are casually surfing the web at work, spend a little time checking out everyone's LinkedIn profiles, Facebook pages, and Twitter feeds. You will find out 90% of what you need to know about people on social media. Make mental notes of these things when you are interacting and use this material when the time is right. Additionally, you should be taking inventory on your co-workers as you walk around the office to introduce yourself. Pay attention to family photos, vacation pictures, and team posters.

When Mike first started working at a technology company in Pennsylvania, he had a manager who hired him and appeared to like him initially, but she was very short and critical of a lot of what he was doing. He knew that he was in the "prove yourself" phase, but he just felt like they were from two different worlds. He had to figure out how to connect with her so that he could focus on his job and advance his career. Mike learned that she had just become a new mom and her husband was an avid Pittsburgh football fan. One day, he was late for work taking care of his son and when he got into the office, Mike didn't realize that he had missed an important meeting. His boss was obviously frustrated. He told her that his kid had an accident in the car and he had to return home to clean it up. Instead of scolding him, she related to his issue and proceeded to tell him her diaper explosion stories about her kids. A couple of days later, Mike came in on Monday morning with a big smile on his face. Noticing this, his boss asked him about his enthusiastic demeanor, and he told her that he was excited that Pittsburgh beat Baltimore. He even threw in how much he hated Baltimore. She smiled, and said she and her husband absolutely loves Pittsburgh! She talked to him about the times they used to go to the games in Pittsburgh and drink beers in the freezing cold.

After those two encounters, Mike noticed that she was far more willing to talk to him and give him the inside track on a lot of things that were happening in the office. She felt more connected to him because they shared the same interests. She also paid more attention to the work that he was doing and supported Mike when he had challenging issues.

It may seem manipulative to some people, but it's necessary for you to go the extra mile to form the relationship from the beginning. The intent is not to be deceiving, but to build the bridge of common ground and comfort. Once you establish that, you will eventually find additional connections when the person opens up to you more and becomes comfortable. You will then have a more organically developed relationship. Simply lying to people to form these relationships is not a best practice.

It's like when a guy meets a woman. He wants to find common ground to connect with her. For example, imagine that his love interest loves Jazz music. The man will use his love of Jazz to generate a relationship based on their mutual interest. Once he gets the conversation going about Jazz, the woman opens up, she gets to know him, and he can now build on additional things that they have in common. However, if he lies about his interest in Jazz and gets caught, he could lose the girl forever.

So you need to be careful how you form these relationships. If you try to fake it, you have to stick to that false script indefinitely, and it doesn't always end well when the truth comes out.

Johnny X worked for a technology firm and he had a boss that loved to play golf. During major golf tournaments, the boss would come in with his red polo and black pants. He'd always have one of his monitors on the sports channel. Almost each day, he would sit in his large cubical, wear a wireless headset, and he would putt a golf ball into a coffee can during his conference calls. Johnny X would often go to his boss's cubical area to ask a question or get something approved. He would ignore Johnny X, and at best, point at his headphones and continue putting.

He really wouldn't talk to anyone, but Johnny X figured out a way to connect with him.

Back at home, Johnny X did a little research about the sport of golf. He learned everything that he could. He learned about the up and coming golf tournaments, the best players, and even learned some of the terminology. The next day, he came into the office and walked up to his boss right before their 10 a.m. call. He asked him who he thought would win the latest major tournament. He noticed his boss perked up. He sat back in his chair, flipped his putter over his right shoulder, and began talking about the tournament, who he thought would win, and about the time he actually went to that tournament a few years back.

As the call was about to start, Johnny X squeezed in an approval for a project budget and his boss happily signed off. As Johnny X walked back to his desk, he told his boss that maybe he'll go out and play a round with him and his buddies sometime. His boss gave him a high five as he put his headset on to start the conference call. Johnny X's plan had worked and he won the day.

Well, that victory was short-lived. Every time Johnny X would come into the office, his boss looked for him to talk about golf. It became an everyday thing. It got to the point where Johnny X had to do research the night before work and prepare what he was going to say to his boss about the latest golf tournament. The wheels fell off when Johnny X's boss tried to pressure him into joining his country club. With all the conversations they had, they made his boss feel like it would be a great idea to play on the weekends with him.

Johnny X couldn't afford it and he actually thought golf was even more unbearable since he had been forcing himself to watch it each day. Johnny X's boss got tired of him making excuses, so one day he paid for him to join the club for a month so that they could go golfing. Johnny X had plans to go to a big college rivalry football game that weekend, but he felt pressured to go since his boss had already spent the money.

Johnny X's goal of getting closer to his boss had worked, but he realized he wasn't willing to go all the way with this golf adventure. Against the wishes of his wife and his buddies he was going to the game with, he decided to go with his boss to play golf. He lost the money on his great football tickets and was disappointed to miss the game of the year. He also had to borrow a set of golf clubs from his buddy because he didn't own any. He knew that he dug himself into a hole, and he created a plan to dig himself out of it.

About three holes into their game, Johnny X faked a back injury driving on a par 4 hole. He dropped to his knees and acted like a refrigerator fell on his back. His boss and the two other men that they were playing with bought it and let him go back to the club house to rest. His boss came in, sat next to him on the couch, and told him that he could go home and rest.

Life back at the office consisted of Johnny X saying his good mornings and continuing to fake his slight back discomfort. The golf conversations became less and less until they stopped altogether. Their relationship basically went back to normal with a nod and dry wave. Johnny X realized that his boss had called his bluff and he couldn't answer the bell.

This is like when a guy tells a woman that he loves musicals, then he finds himself watching *Grease* or buying tickets to *Hamilton*.

The moral of the story is to make sure if you're going to bait and switch a business relationship, you need to make sure that you are willing to go all the way with it.

We've spent a lot of time talking about management and getting to know them to help your career along. However, there are some people lower on the totem pole that you definitely have to meet. Some of these people will be your greatest assets in the long run.

VIPs You Must Meet at the Office

Executive administrative assistants. The executive administrative assistants are the most important people that you should want to meet. They are the gate-keepers for everything regarding management, important meetings, and events. They control the schedules of the most important people in the company, they sit in the most exclusive meetings, and have the most facetime with senior leadership. Having administrative assistants (also known as admins, but don't call them that) on your team provides you opportunity to get on your manager's packed schedule, get an advocate to make sure your senior leadership knows how good of a job you're doing, or lets you know when some big news is about to drop. In a lot of cases, they also have the ear of the senior managers that they support. They are like the best friends of the man or woman that you want to date and your success can sometimes hinge on their opinion of you.

You should always make a concerted effort to befriend the executive administrators of the senior managers that you will be working with and always spend a little time making small talk with them. You should always take care of them. Buy their kids' candy drive treats or get them a card for Administrative Professionals Day (formerly known as Secretary Appreciation Day). Make sure they know you respect and appreciate what they do. The more comfortable that they are with you, the more likely they are to share information with you.

One of the first rules to *not* break when interacting with them is to know their correct title. Never call an executive administrative assistant an "admin." Some people have worked hard for their titles and like the distinction. If someone is a senior manager and they are referred to as just a "manager," you will be called out on it. Make sure that you never call them "secretaries" or simply "assistants." Remember, all titles matter.

Security guards and parking attendants. This group is so underrated. The security department and/or the parking attendant of a company are the eyes and ears of the facility that are always on duty. They have different relationships with management than you do. It's very casual, and often they catch employees walking to their cars, talking on their cell phones, and being informal.

Once they are on your side, the knowledge that they have about things that are happening, is golden. They can let you know which big wigs are in town, when the boss leaves for the day, and who's vandalizing your car.

The quickest way to develop a relationship with security is to treat them with respect. Although the typical security guard is a part-time officer that in most cases doesn't have a gun and can't arrest you, treat him as if he really is a police officer. You should never look down on them, nor refer to them as rent-a-cops or Top Flight Security of the World, as some will do. Instead, acknowledge them every day and learn their names. Ask them what's going on at the site for the day. Every now and then, act like you need their help with something. After feeling really important to you, they will run to the opportunity to tell you some information that they think is significant or classified. This is part of developing your interpersonal skills.

Unfortunately, the reality is that everyone will not treat them like you do. Some high profile people feel comfortable speaking freely around them because they typically don't view them as part of company personnel. Additionally, they don't anticipate that other employees have close relationships with the security guards. Because of this, the high profilers casually express their real feelings about their colleagues or plans for the future without fear of it leaking out.

Having your own team of security guards looking out for you or just keeping their ears open makes them a valuable asset. The key to getting information from security guards is that you can never reveal your sources once they give you this data. You must do whatever you can to protect them from the blowback of telling you a secret.

Janitors. Unlike security, these are the eyes and ears on the ground in the trenches. They know who's working late, who's having after office conversations, and what they are talking about. Typically, janitors are treated like they are on the bottom of the food chain. They usually don't receive any acknowledgement except for a dry "hello" or a "thank you" after they dump the trash bin. Executives, in my experience, often talk about things in their presence as if they are a picture on the wall. It's not a disrespectful thing. In most cases, everyone is just so busy and the service employees don't have any impact on the subjects at hand.

My mother told me as a child to always treat everyone with respect, so it's an attribute that I possess naturally from my upbringing. However, in terms of a business relationship, it's wise to treat these people with as much respect that you would give a vice-president or a CEO. This group is privy to so much information. If they don't know who you are, or what your interests are, you'll never have access to that valuable intelligence.

As a program manager at a big IT company, I had an awesome relationship with the janitor who came by once a day to empty my trash can. Her name was Ms. Ella. We'd get to the office around the same time every day, so I would make small talk with her in the parking lot on the way into the building if we were walking up together. After a few months, she knew what I actually did for the company and who my boss was. I knew about her family and her daughter that was playing basketball in middle school. One afternoon, I ran into her in the supermarket with her family; I stopped to say hello and to meet her kids. Ever since then, we had an even stronger connection and continued to make small talk conversations whenever we saw each other in the building.

One day, she was working during a senior staff meeting in the executive conference room. As she was cleaning, she overheard the Senior Vice President say that he is planning on laying off dozens of employees based on certain criteria at the end of the quarter. She was eager to share this information with me. She also admitted that my name came up specifically. This revelation not only allowed me to change course on what I was working on, but it got me promoted.

Cafeteria workers. Some of the best gossip happens in the cafeteria over a meal. Just like the janitors, people in the office act as if the cafeteria workers aren't there. They don't have any reason to engage them unless they are making them a sandwich. However, this couldn't be further from the truth. The cafeteria is one of the few places that you will encounter cross-functional team and department interaction.

In prison, one of the most important places to interact is the chow hall. Besides being in the yard, breakfast and lunchtime in prison is where a lot of deals and exchanges go down. Some of the most important people in that environment are the cafeteria workers. They get to touch everyone in the room with their guards down. People are free and give up a lot of information and gossip over a meal.

At one of Johnny X's former jobs, there was a huge cafeteria with two sections to get food from. There was a self-service area known as the cold side and the grill side known as the hot side. The Head Cook Rico was an old school guy in his late 60s who really loved cooking on the grill. He would be playing his old Motown music on the radio, while singing and talking to people as they placed orders. While people were waiting on their hamburgers to get fried, Rico would ask his customer, "Hey what's going on today?"

In most cases the person would download their entire morning. All their issues, concerns, and ill feelings about other people. It was like people couldn't wait to gossip with Rico each day. Johnny X started to go in the hot line more often just to listen in on what was going on. It was better than cable news.

Executive/management advocate/support. Having an advocate in senior management is great to have and very hard to get. It's difficult because given your position, you may not have access to senior-level managers or spend enough time with them to form a real relationship. However, if you are able to, it's highly recommended. Go as high as you can up the food chain and start by seeking one of them out as a mentor. That usually gets your foot in the door.

The advantages are obvious. One, you have an advocate that literally has the power to change your career. Two, you get to pick their brain about management and the direction the company is going in. Sometimes when executive level management leaves the company for greener pastures, they want to take their own team to the new destination.

Often in professional sports, when a coordinator gets a head coaching job, they bring in their own staff of people that have worked under them before.

The same rules apply in Corporate America. So not only are you helping secure your future in your company with your advocate, but you also may be opening up a new opportunity down the road. Often times in business, people end up reconnecting with an old boss later on. It's a great ace to have in your back pocket.

Now that you know who some of your allies are and how to leverage those relationships, it's time to meet the pieces on the other side of the chess board. In fact, it's more important to know your enemies better than you know your teammates. Your offense is 100 times better if you understand the strengths and weakness of the defense that you are facing. Let's spend some time learning about who your enemies are and how to best deal with them.

There are always people to watch out for. As the dynamics change in the office, friends can become foes, peers can become your manager, and haters will always be looking for the right time to strike against you. While some people and their motives aren't easy to detect from the start, there are some types of people that show their true colors early. It's a good idea to watch out for them and not let them in too close.

Office Personality Types to Watch Out For

The "Brown-Noser/Policy Police." This person is very dangerous because they are willing to say or do anything in order to be in management's good graces. Their motives aren't always self-serving in the name of advancing themselves. They will sometimes throw you under the bus just because. The good news is that these types of people usually make themselves known early on and often. The best way to deal with this kind of a person is to always be prepared for the worst around them. For example, being put on the spot by anticipating their angles. Just be prepared to address what they dish out.

The "Wanna-be Executive." This type of person is slightly easier to deal with. It's clear what they want and what's important to them. This person can be easily swayed by people who appear to be an asset to their cause, and therefore, they avoid conflict that could derail their career path. The dangerous part about them is when they view you as a threat. This is one of the reasons you don't express your goals and ambitions to everyone.

Given the right or most desperate situation, this person becomes the brown-noser—only more covertly than your typical ones. The best course of action is to play it cool with them and act as if you are in support of their goal. Sometimes they actually succeed and you don't want to be on the wrong side of history if they become your boss or some type of senior leader.

The "Hating Snitch." This person is different from the Brown-noser because their motives aren't for selfish reasons. At least with a Brown-noser, you know that they are in it for themselves and are blinded by the hope of coming up. You would simply be a casualty of their advancement. The Hating Snitch just doesn't want to see you come up. The Hater will take anything that you do and make it out to be a bad thing. They discredit your success, whether you are following policy or improving the lives of your colleagues.

The best way to deal with a Hating Snitch is to avoid them at all costs and to keep unavoidable interactions with them as surface level as possible. Don't provide any unnecessary ammunition to your haters. The key to remember about this type of person is that you must always remember that your hater will always exist and hate on your success. The second key is that your haters will never be converted. Once a hater, always a hater. Never let your guard down and fall for an act of kindness or fleeting compliment on a conference call. It's a set up. The *only* exception to their non-converting hating mindsets, is when you are choosing to depart from a company. If you're leaving, there is a possibility that the Hating Snitch no longer sees you as a threat and no longer chooses to hate you, but again, don't let your guard down.

The "Cool Co-worker." The Cool Co-Worker can be deceiving because they are sitting back in the cut listening and soaking up all of the information being shared around them. They are the ultimate poker player because they don't behave in a manner that would immediately raise any red flags. However, they may be plotting to destroy you or to take the very thing that you are working so hard for, whether it's a project or a promotion.

The Cool Co-Worker is another person that you keep at bay. Enjoy the peace and harmony of their coolness and perceived attitude. Enjoy the great conversations about what they did over the weekend. Accept the compliments and perceived support that you are given. However, never forget that you are on the battlefield and that you are supposed to be on at all times. Do not let your guard down ever.

The "Complainer." The Complainer is… how can I say it? *Annoying.* The Complainer is bad to be around due to their negative energy and perception in the office. A lot of managers and program managers choose to not have these types of people on their team because, in most cases, the complaining becomes unbearable. You have to be careful to not be associated with them or be identified as a Complainer yourself.

The positive side of the Complainer cannot be ignored either. They offer a wealth of feedback that can benefit you if you use it correctly. In a lot of cases, the Complainer has valid points and isn't afraid to express them. This is very good information to have because when the opportunity presents itself, you are able to offer up the solution to their issues.

Stand clear of being the side-kick of the Complainer, but you should always milk them for their information. The best way to get their data is in private or on the sideline. Let them complain to you one-on-one after a meeting is over or at lunch off site. On the other hand, never, ever, ever share complaints with them. One of the worst positions that you can put yourself in is to utter your grievances to a Complainer who has no problem airing out their own issues. Not only will they tell everyone else, but they usually tell the story wrong.

The "Super Senior." This person has been at the company forever with no promotion or job title change, but don't be fooled by this. They have seen it all and heard it all when it comes down to the company. They have survived new CEOs, mergers, and layoffs. They are battle-tested and have all the respect of everyone that comes after them. The Super Senior usually has a lot of influence in the office over co-workers and managers alike.

These employees are often sought after by HR, Corporate Communications, or other areas of management to help promote or support an announcement or policy change among the other team members. You always want to know who these people are and figure out how to leverage their influence. More importantly, you don't want to get on their bad side. This is one of the easiest ways to get the population to turn against you.

The "Paranoid Co-worker." The Paranoid is constantly in fear of losing their jobs. They always speak on every layoff rumor, company re-organization, and buy-out. They usually assume that management is always out to get them specifically. They often paint themselves as the victim and try to convince you that everyone is always in constant danger.

They over talk and unwittingly give up important information. They are often manipulated by alphas in the office being motivated by fear and the hope that they will stay in good graces with the people who are perceived to have power.

The "Relative." Whether they are over qualified with a wealth of experience and multiple advanced degrees, or they are the drunken frat boy, college drop-out who just got out of rehab for his addiction to prescription drugs, you need to beware. Nepotism in the workplace is a recipe for disaster when you're forced to go up against the tribal bond of a colleague that's related to management in any way. You are better off just trying to befriend this person and develop a decent working relationship. At best, they could have favor in you and possibly advocate for you at a later date. At the very worst, they can hate your guts and use their leverage to do you in. Sadly, ethics and following the guidelines of the conflict of interest policies don't matter.

When Johnny X was a teenager, he played on a select basketball team with a coach who had his son on the roster. Do you think that Johnny and his teammates could go at the coach's son without any retribution? In a perfect world, yes. In the real world... not so much.

The Relative is dangerous because the playing field is titled like a bootleg boxing match in the champ's hometown. You'll never win. Just observe them and take mental notes of what they say and do in the office. Get an idea of what type of talent they have, their weaknesses, and their influence in the office. Most importantly, try not to get caught in their cross-hairs.

Now that you know about the type of people that you should align with and/or watch out for, you need to put people in their appropriate categories. The people that you put into these categories aren't stuck there, but you need to be 100% sure that they are worthy of being moved. The terms used below are not the standard definitions of these words, but as they relate to being in the sphere of Corporate America. Most colleagues can be separated into four categories: co-worker, friends, enemies, and the scout team.

Co-worker. Your co-workers are people that you have a professional relationship with. They are either managers, peers, or subordinates that you work for within the same company. Co-workers are just everyday people around you that go about their day doing their work. You may not necessarily have any type of relationship that you can categorize just yet. Although you may not, this doesn't mean that everything is all good. Always be professional, polite, and treat them with the utmost respect, but remember that you don't know them on a level to be able to categorize them just yet.

Remain protective of yourself and your best interest. It's like going to play pick-up basketball with a group of guys you never played with before. Don't assume that they can't shoot, give up wide open jumpers, and then realize after you lose that they can actually shoot the lights out. Play them honest, respect the drive, dish, or shot. You can then adjust after you find out what they can do or once you find out what kind of player they are. The weakest looking guy can be the dirtiest player. Same rules apply in the office.

Friends. The office friends are colleagues that you may either work with directly or just share an office space and hang out together socially. These are your buddies that you spend time with in the break room, the gym, or conferences.

Friends are the people that you can trust to a certain extent. Remember, friends are level one surface range of discretion. They are good to have lunch with, detox from the stress of the office with, and lean on for help in certain situations. You can get them birthday cakes, Christmas cards, and let them borrow your phone charger. You know, friend stuff. You trust them like a cellmate.

Be careful about putting colleagues in this category. Just because you share a few laughs with someone and helped someone out on a project, doesn't make you friends. Believe it or not, some people pose as your friend with the intent of covertly destroying you and elevating themselves. It's okay to be nice and have a good time, but always keep in mind that you are in the workplace. The game goes on whether you think that you are playing or not.

In a lot of cases, people may come into the company with a person who was a friend before a colleague. This is tricky because although they were friends first, the law of the office still applies. Business comes first all of the time. Not in the sense that you cut your best friend's throat to get ahead, but to protect yourself from your friend and to preserve the relationship.

Your friend knows everything about you. They have an inside track to you that no one in the office has. Not only do you have to worry about them betraying you, but you also have to worry about the possibility of them giving up intelligence without you even knowing.

Mike was working for a government contractor as a technical writer in the same department as his buddy Greg with whom he played basketball with three times a week. They became friends over the course of a year, having played on the same team in a recreational league. One day, Greg told him in the gym's sports bar that he had applied for a job in the communications department as a technical writer. Mike was excited because he was already a senior technical writer and he thought that it would be great to have his basketball buddy on the writing team.

Once Greg got the job on the strength of Mike's recommendation, Greg went into the department doing pretty good work and seamlessly transitioned into a valuable team member. He and Mike were not only hanging out at the gym, but they were also hanging out at lunch at the office and even double-dated with their spouses. They were like Mike Lowry and Marcus Burnett from the 1995 movie *Bad Boys*.[8]

Everything was great until about a year later when Greg decided he wanted to be more than a junior writer. Coincidentally, the communications department had an opening for a communications director. Mike was the most senior person applying for the job, but Greg felt that he was qualified to put his name in the hat as well. Although both of them had applied for the job, they decided to not talk about it to each other as sort of a brotherhood pact. It was sort of a situation where they both resigned to the idea, "may the best person win." What the two of them did not realize was that there was another junior associate in the running for the job. Her name was Maddy, and she was one of the fan favorites of the communications office, but her experience was shaky at best.

Over the next few weeks, Maddy reached out to Greg to ask him questions about Mike. Greg knew that Maddy had a few connections with the communications team, so he thought he could use her as a pawn to build his chances by giving a little intelligence on his buddy. What he didn't know is that she was on the hunt as well. So Greg continued to dry-snitch on Mike about how he snuck out early on certain afternoons, how he created presentations, and that his ultimate career goal was to leave communications after two years to pursue a career in program management. Greg was in full Benedict Arnold mode at this point.

Maddy took that valuable information and not only used it to denigrate Mike, but also used his best practices as her own during her interview. When Mike went in for his interview, he received a cold, short set of responses to the questions he had and a disinterest in the answers that he responded with. The hiring manager heard from two candidates using Mike's information and best practices, plus the revelation of his career plans had turned them off. In the end, Maddy got the job and she kept Mike as the senior writer. She had to; she wasn't able fully do her job without him. Mike was so disappointed, and he couldn't understand why he was passed over when he was the most qualified.

Two months later, Greg was laid off and Mike was even more depressed. Not only did he lose out on the promotion, but he also lost his work buddy. One day, Maddy went to Mike in a staff meeting before everyone in the room arrived. She asked him about the status of a late writing assignment, and off topic, he responded by saying he missed working with Greg. Maddy understood, but she mentioned that Mike should be careful about how he chooses his friends. She explained that she heard some disparaging remarks about him through the "proverbial office grapevine." She spoke of things that only Greg knew from personal conversations that they had while hanging out. She didn't mention that she used them, but just that she "heard" them.

Mike was bamboozled by his own buddy. Greg attempted to cut a side deal with Maddy like G-Money did with Scotty behind Nino Brown's back in *New Jack City*.[9]

Mike began to replay all the conversations that he and Greg had. It made him sick to his stomach. He realized that business and friendship don't always mix.

You can have a friend in the office, but you would have to be guarded at all times with your career information. When it comes down to it, "friend" and "enemy" can become synonymous.

Enemies. Enemies are just what they are characterized as. The ones you know hate you and want your spot. Enemies are the people who work to destroy your reputation, steal your work, or just make it difficult for you in the office. The motives aren't always clear, but they don't matter because they are not in your best interest. Once you put a person in this category, you *almost never* take them out. There is only *one* exception to this rule: if you leave your current job, you're no longer a threat to that enemy, so technically they would no longer *be* your enemy. You probably wouldn't hang out with them for fun on the weekends, but you more than likely will no longer be a hated target either. Nevertheless, as long as you're working in the same office with an established enemy, they can never be removed from this category.

When Jermaine was asked to spearhead a small communications team by the division manager, he was also asked to lead a big program that the organization wanted to implement. The communications team was full of moderately experienced professionals that weren't thrilled about a new person leading the team. However, once Jermaine launched the program, it became very successful and he appointed different people on the team to lead their own projects within the program. It was a way to provide them a little more job security and to build comradery amongst one another. He thought that he was doing something good for people who were nervous about new leadership coming in and taking over. Jermaine also thought that it would win over a few individuals who felt he was inexperienced.

At the end of the year, the division manager left the company and upper management was looking to hire a replacement. Most people in the office thought that Jermaine would get consideration for the job since he was basically already doing the job of the absent division manager as well.

What Jermaine found out was that two people on the team that he helped prevent from being laid off, were secretly meeting with another colleague and providing him information about the team, what they were working on, and the new strategies that Jermaine was using to make the program so strong. They also advocated for their other colleague to get the job, which he did. To add insult to injury, Jermaine was asked to train the new division manager on the final few strategies that the moles were providing him. That was a great lesson for Jermaine.

You will never fully win over your enemies. You can earn the most basic forms of respect and professionalism, but you'll never have their full support.

Scout Team. These people can be members of all four categories. However, they are valuable assets to your cause. The scout team is a group of people that are part of your company, but people that you can use to test the waters and/or find out how things will play out if certain actions are taken. This is not meant to be construed as manipulating people or setting them up to fail; it's just being able to leverage other people's experiences in order to understand outcomes, whether they result in success or disaster.

In professional football, the scout team consists of the players that don't play in the games on Sunday, but are used by the players who will play. The scout team mirrors or imitates the opponent's key players to see how the starters will respond to certain situations on the field. If there is a running quarterback on the scout team that is running past all of the starting defense, there is a problem, and practice is the time to correct it.

You have probably heard that experience is the best teacher, but in some cases, someone else's experience is the best teacher.

Nathan saw his neighbors grow up in a household where everyone was living a life of crime. There was a family of four: husband, wife, and two teenage sons. The man's name was Mr. Clark, or Mr. Mac as he was known in the street. Mr. Mac sold drugs, his wife was addicted to them, and both his sons sold for him. After about 5-6 years, Mr. Mac was killed by a rival drug gang in the neighborhood, while his two sons went to prison for selling drugs and murder. His wife ended up on the street where she turned to prostitution to get drugs and make a living. It was a harsh reality of what that drug life led to, but it was enough for Nathan to know that it wasn't the life he ever wanted for himself. Drugs would never be part of his life.

Just like in football and Nathan's experience, this is the same way that the scout team works for you in the workplace. There are people in your company that are making power moves. Sometimes good moves, sometimes bad. Pay attention to what's going on. Watch how people try to assert themselves, watch how arguments play out, watch how people act around others they claim to hate, and most importantly, watch how people respond to pressure or adversity.

One of the most critical qualities that you can learn about people is what their triggers are and how they respond when they are pressed. The beauty of having the scout team is the ability to get these data points without having to jump into the fire yourself. Anyone can be part of your scout team. It could be friends, enemies, team members, or anyone that engages within the parameters of your circle. Just be sure to not tell them that you are mentally documenting their interactions as reconnaissance work for your own personal use later on.

In addition, you need to realize that *you* are on someone else's scout team. When you can help it, don't conduct business in front of an audience. Don't allow people to get game off of your hard work or difficult situations. Just like in life, try to be a little mysterious when it comes to how you really feel and how you go about getting certain tasks done.

Don't be so predictable that people will scout you and put the pieces together so easily. Only do this if it is part of an alternative plan. In fact, the only time that this would be good is if you want to throw people off of your true feelings or motives about something. Sometimes you may feel the need to "lose a battle to win the war" or "play a sucker to catch a sucker." You have to be really careful with doing things like this because if it's executed incorrectly, it could come back to bite you in the end.

Lastly, don't share your research with anyone. This is for your use and benefit only. Besides, in this game, knowledge is truly power. You don't want to give away this valuable information for free, nor do you not want to risk the possibility of people knowing you have a mental or physical dossier on them or the situations at hand.

Post-Game Takeaways:

✗ Five skills professionals should have in the workplace: (1) be self-aware, (2) be able to read and translate nonverbal communication, (3) be respectful and understanding of others, (4) be a great communicator, and (5) be an active listener.

✗ Data to keep to yourself: personal business, opinions of colleagues, and business plans.

✗ VIPs to meet: executive administrative assistants, security guards/parking attendants, janitors, cafeteria workers, and executive management advocate/support.

✗ Office personality types: the "Brown-noser/Policy Police," the "Wanna-be Executive," the "Hating Snitch," the "Cool Co-worker," the "Complainer," the "Super Senior," the "Paranoid Co-worker," and the "Relative."

✗ Colleague categories: co-worker, friends, enemies, and scout team.

*** GAME TIP ***

While racism, sexism, and other isms' exist, everything that happens doesn't always point to that accusation. If you experience discrimination in any type of way, you should by all means report it through the appropriate channels within your company. However, you need to watch out for people in the workplace that harp on these type of topics in the office. For one reason, you don't want to involve yourself in someone else's legal proceedings, and secondly, you don't want to have the reputation of stirring controversies that aren't there. If you meet someone like this in the office, it's alright to listen to their complaint the first time, but encourage them to report it and keep it moving.

*** GAME TIP ***

Identifying and developing a relationship with influencers of people in the office is always great when you are trying to get information from people or to get things done. Influencers can be anyone in your office that either intimidates, inspires, or irritates certain people around you. Knowing who they are and how they influence your other colleagues can be a valuable thing to have under your belt. It's very important to pay attention to what people say around you when you appear to not be listening. Soak it all up; it'll be priceless later.

*** GAME TIP ***

If your office has social areas such as cafeterias, gyms, or common seating spaces, make sure to spend some time in these places at some point each week. These are great places to form relationships with people that you may run into all the time for lunch breaks or workout sessions. You'll also get to find out who are really friends with each other.

Playbook Notes

CHAPTER 5
COMMUNICATIONS

Pre-Game Analysis:

- ✗ How to prepare for and conduct yourself during meetings.

- ✗ How to handle social events.

- ✗ How to manage electronic communications.

Communication is the greatest asset that you will have in your arsenal when it comes to building your brand or protecting it. The poorest, least attractive man can get the finest woman if he has the right amount of charisma and the gift of gab. The same goes for professionals in the workplace. The key to success is not only being able to talk the talk, but to know when to talk it and how to represent yourself in certain situations.

Most people think that their interpersonal skills are up to date, but this is where most fall short or become a victim. As it's been stated, the game is on at all times. So never assume that it is all good during what seems to be personal office conversation with a colleague. Communication is one of the biggest areas to play the office game.

People look at how you conduct yourself in these business situations to judge your level of professionalism and expertise. The challenge in today's work environment is generational, cultural, and regional. There are some traditional ways to conduct yourself in the office from the way you dress, the way you treat superiors, and even in the way people collaborate.

Traditional practices have shifted slightly depending on where you are located in the world. For example, the dress code is really relaxed in Austin, Texas where men wear jeans and T-shirts to work on Mondays, where in the Washington, D.C. area, people wear suits and ties. Technology has also had a tremendous impact on how we communicate. With many meetings happening via Conference call, just being in the room doesn't give you credit for participating. You now have to chime in on the call to show that you're collaborating.

Additionally, there is a big gap in social interaction practices between baby boomers and Generation Z. Sharing the workspace with the old school generation that wants to speak face-to-face and handle issues head-on is competing with a generation that would rather avoid talking to other people by using text message with short-hand script and emojis. There is no right or wrong way to approach these dynamics, but the person who can master them both and bridge the communication gaps will come out on top. While there are definitely differences to overcome, as no corporate environment or culture is the same, there are some fundamental attributes that remain consistent to the basic tenants of professionalism. Learn, know, and understand what those are, and you will be able to adapt to any situation that you find yourself in professionally.

Face-to-Face Meetings

For F2F meetings, it is important to never be late if you can help it. Make sure you know where the conference room is before you are due to arrive. It's good to get there at least five minutes before the meeting starts so that you can get settled, drink some water, and catch some of the meeting small talk between the managers or the brown-nosers.

If you are presenting, it's good to get there at least 20-30 minutes early. You will need to make sure the presentation deck is working and that there isn't any last minute changes you need to make to the content. Get preliminary feedback on your ideas before the rest of the group comes to the meeting.

Be prepared. Before any meeting, it is imperative that you assess what you need to have for the current meeting at hand. If you're presenting, make sure that your material is what your bosses and/or team is looking for. In addition, you should rehearse what you want to say, or at least, how your presentation will flow.

This is only the beginning. You should anticipate what questions you are going to get and be prepared to answer them. Managers and executives like it when an employee shows some initiative to resolve issues. It shows them that you have leadership skills. Be sure to understand the past chain of events and how you got to the current phase of your project or discussion. That's why it is very important to keep meticulous notes and not rely solely on the meeting minutes.

Dress the part. In this new age, we have become relaxed about our appearance in the workplace. In the early days of Corporate America, people wore suits, ties, and even jackets to work on a daily basis, unless they were forced to wear some type of uniform. Fast forward to the present day. Some people still hold on to the traditional dress code, and only let loose on casual Friday with their favorite jeans and a football jersey.

However, in the wake of the Googles, Facebooks, and call centers of the world, the next generation has given into a more informal dress code. The idea that we should be able to wear what inspires us, or what we are more comfortable in, has become the philosophy of the moment when it comes to how we look at work.

We see this phenomenon in various parts of our lives. People are wearing jeans and T-shirts to funerals. They are wearing pajamas to class on college campuses all over the United States.

There once was a guy who came into our office in a full scuba gear outfit for Halloween when we were having a small masquerade party. It's often blamed on the Hollywood Elite and how their dress code varies along the entire spectrum at red carpet events. However, you have to remember that you are not a million-dollar Hollywood heavyweight. You're trying to dress to impress and promote your brand, while also playing the game with the cool kids on the playground.

This isn't about being old-fashioned and dictating to people what they should be wearing, but it is about the idea of knowing how to dress for the situation. Knowing what to wear, when, and more importantly, what not to wear is sometimes the difference between working in a new corner office, and working at the old corner store.

One morning, Johnny X was assigned to go to a meeting with a few members of the military personnel and a couple of government officials with his General Manager. He knew that he had to dress his best to be amongst this crowd. Johnny X wanted to let his boss know that he could up his game from the basic khakis and white button-down shirts that he was wearing every day to the office. So he went home the night before and went straight to the left side of the closet where Johnny X kept all of his well-to-do garments. He picked out some navy blue slacks, gray blazer, a powder blue shirt, and a paisley tie and pocket square to match.

He even threw in the argyle socks with silver cufflinks, tie pin, and a black belt with a silver buckle that all matched the silver buckles on his black faux alligator Kenneth Cole shoes. This was the best outfit in his closet, hands down.

When Johnny X got to the office, he strutted in slowly with his black computer bag thrown over his left shoulder so that his right arm would be free to shake hands. He even noticed that his computer bag matched his shoes. Man, was he killing it that morning—so he thought.

As Johnny X started shaking hands and saying good morning, the room started moving in slow motion like the fighting scenes in the *Matrix*.[10]

He started looking around the room as he gave these half-hearted handshakes and realized that every single man in that room had on a white shirt and a basic solid color tie. There were no paisleys, no tie clips, no cufflinks, and certainly no fake alligator shoes. There was only him in a room full of conservative government and military personnel. Johnny X looked like a Southern Baptist Minister about to preach the revival sermon. He shrank into his chair and logged into his laptop to get ready for the meeting. He could feel the eyes on his powder blue Mississippi pimp-looking dress shirt, so he removed the tie clip to bring some normalcy to his ensemble. His boss walked over and glanced at his shirt and tie. He started the meeting with his chin tucked so that he was looking over the rim of his glasses.

Johnny X felt uncomfortable the entire day, so much so that he felt like every time he said something, people discredited his answers just because of what he was wearing. During the lunch break, his GM told him that he looked great, fresh out of GQ Magazine. However, he was told to scale it back in the future, and to buy 10 white dress shirts because he would be going out to their offices on his own to run the program.

His GM taught Johnny X a valuable lesson about knowing his audience, understanding the culture of their environment, and assimilating to make them feel comfortable about working with him. In their environment, it's almost understood that they are supposed to wear dark pants and white shirts every day.

Johnny X understood what his GM meant in that situation, but he learned even more from that experience. He thought about the times he went to job interviews and wasn't dressed for the part. He had plans after the interview and wanted to be comfortable for his own activities.

Johnny X realized that dressing the part is not about just wearing what societal norms dictate, but he would need to do some homework about where he would be going and who he would be around.

It's a best practice to do this research because it's hard to change a bad first impression. If you're not sure, it's always a good thing to over dress in a way that you can dress it down if you need to. It's easier to go down than it is to go up. It's a good idea to keep a spare choice in the car when possible. I keep a polo and a dress shirt and tie in my office because I never know when I'll need to switch it up.

Be confident. If you have done your homework before your meeting, you should be oozing with confidence as you present your material. Of course, being confident doesn't mean being arrogant, but just being poised throughout your presentation. Make sure that you are smiling and looking everyone in the eyes as you scan the room. You will have some people in the room who want to elevate themselves or make you look bad by poking holes in your presentation or your responses. Always maintain your composure in these moments.

Remember that you will have an opportunity after the presentation is over to talk to this person offline. Don't let them see you sweat. Even if you make a mistake, just own it and continue presenting. Believe it or not, people will respect you more if you deal with it like a pro and move on.

Be positive; solutions-oriented. Sometimes these meetings become very contentious. It's important for you to maintain your composure. Instead of being equally combative, you can be firm, but still positive. When someone is interrupting you or being obtuse, simply pause, acknowledge what they are saying, and then transition back into what your point is. Instead of pointing fingers, throw out a few solutions. If your manager is there, ask them what the desired outcome is and then offer your solutions. Refer to previous experiences on resolving this type of issue and offer to lead the group out of it. Senior managers will remember moments like this. People who can be firm, but solutions-oriented are coveted by senior managers and executives who don't want to get their hands dirty.

The person in the room that is able to listen to everyone's arguments and complaints, and appear to be the voice of reason, will always be valued. Many people will put themselves out there as self-proclaimed experts, and that is fine. Let them be the experts. The real champion is the person that can put it all together and make the team or the plan work.

Social Events

Social events can be a little tricky because you have to strike a healthy balance between being professional and getting loose with the co-workers. Although all events are not exactly the same, there are some basic actions that you can take to make sure that you represent yourself well. There are huge benefits to attending social events for professional purposes. It's a short-term investment that can give you long-term gains.

You have to remember that although this is a "social engagement," this is still a business meeting. Your boss and competition are still in the room, so it's still game on. It is wise to use this time to your advantage to watch people, do everything in moderation, and take mental notes for your scout team work.

Arrive during, leave before it's over. Unlike F2F business meetings in the office, you are not required to be the first person in the room. In fact, you don't want to be unless you're helping to coordinate the event. If you are a guest, you want to be fashionably late so that you can make an entrance to shake hands and scope out the clicks and alliances in the room. You want to be the cool person entering the room as the new shiny leader for everyone to look at. Some people have been in the party for a while and the crowd has already been fatigued by seeing them walk back and forth across the room. There may be some that have asked about you.

On a certain level, your attendance may become anticipated. When you show up to the party, walk in with a smile, shake hands with everyone that comes into your space, and compliment people while scanning the room. Locate the brown-nosers and see whose mingling with who before you make a move to talk to any senior level managers—unless, of course, they approach you first. Remain at the event for about 30-45 minutes if it's a party.

The exception to this rule is if the event is accompanied with a show or a dinner that starts promptly. For formal business dinners, your boss's private events, movies, presentations, and conferences, you definitely want to be there early. If this is the case, please adhere to the F2F meeting rules.

On the other hand, you don't want to be there to shut the party down. There is such a thing called leaving fashionably early. You don't want to be the last person standing at the open bar at 2:00 a.m. with the other drunk guy from Marketing. These are not like your college days when it was cool to still be in the club when the lights came back on. After you have made your rounds in the room and held a few conversations, you should be good to go. Staying at an event about 50% of the scheduled time is good enough unless there is a climatic event, an award presentation, an announcement, or closing remarks that you need to be present for.

Be sure to just have one drink. Although you may think you are a veteran drinker that can hold your liquor, your work events aren't the places to do it. This is the time where you need to be as conservative as possible. If you don't drink, great! If you can't resist, just have one, and make it something that you definitely can handle. Having one drink is okay. You can sip your favorite drink and mingle throughout the room without looking like a lush. The positive image you are portraying is that you are not uptight, but you are also responsible.

Movies often have really funny scenes with people getting drunk at an office Christmas party. You don't want to be one of those people. Colleagues will hold it against you and laugh at you behind your back for the rest of your tenure at that company. You have to remember that you are still on, and people are still watching and judging you. Whether you can hold your liquor or not, your co-workers are already prepared for the moment when they can use your bad behavior at the party to assassinate your character in the office. As everyone knows, being the office drunk is one of the easiest ways to give your brand a black eye.

You want to make sure you compliment the planner and thank them for the invite. This is part of your relationship building process. At some point *during* the event find the planners *of* the event to: (1) show that you came to the event and (2) give them a pat on the back for a job well done. You need to do this for a few reasons. Primarily, you want to secure a positive relationship with the event planner because with the responsibility they have, they are most likely highly connected. Secondly, you may need this person's assistance in the future. If people feel appreciated by you, they are more likely to help you when the time comes. Finally, if it was by invitation, make sure to say "thank you" for being invited. Chances are you will be invited to other events where you can network.

Knowing how to have a conversation at these events is important. We are going to get straight to the point about this topic. This is not the time to keep it real, take a political stance, tell a dirty joke, or gossip about a manager or co-worker. You have two ears and one mouth, so in these situations you want to listen twice as much as you talk. This is the time that you should be a "journalist." Listen and learn about as much as you can about people. Find out their interests, their strengths, weaknesses, and future plans. Make mental notes to yourself and only chime in when asked a question.

There are three tips to follow in order to get through these conversations at social events: (1) don't over-talk, (2) don't change the subject, and (3) don't discuss controversial topics.

Don't over-talk everyone. Don't be the person that everyone avoids at the party because you just won't shut up. People will avoid you like the plague when they see you coming. In doing so, you will find yourself excluded from all of the juicy intelligence. In fact, social event conversations with colleagues are some of the best circles to be a part of. People are relaxed and drinking, and likely to talk more freely than they would in the office. This is a good time to let the motor-mouths talk themselves into oblivion while you smile and nod as the tidal wave of information falls into your lap. Remember, 2/3 of the time goes to listening and 1/3 goes to talking. When you do talk, don't cut anyone off in mid-sentence and don't gossip.

Don't change the subject. If you walk up to a conversation already in progress and there is something else you want to discuss with a particular person in the group, do it later. Make sure that you blend in as part of the group so that people will feel comfortable with you around.

I once sat in a group of senior managers talking about their vacations and the work they were doing for the job while they were out. I thought surely I could chime in and add my two cents about the basketball league I play in on my off days. Wrong! One of the Vice Presidents looked over at me subtly and sent me on an errand to find someone for him. With that gesture, he basically said that I didn't belong with them, and I talked my way out of a bonding moment with the big dogs in our division. Just be a fly on the wall.

Don't discuss controversial topics. This is a really important one. Ethic and compliance, sexual harassment, and employee retaliation suits are all on the table. Do not talk about your religious beliefs, your political party affiliation, what the other party is doing wrong, race relations, and most certainly do not air any dirty laundry about the job.

Johnny X worked for a PR firm in New York that had offices all over the world. The company decided to host an all company meeting in an exotic location. The team narrowed it down to Hawaii where they spent a 3-day conference with everyone from interns to CEOs in attendance. Johnny X struggled a bit because he was new to the company and he had a problem getting new contracts. The contract he was hired to work on for the firm was won by another company and other account executives were typically giving new work to their favorite employees that already worked on their teams before.

Johnny X knew that he was in danger of being laid off if he didn't start logging in billable hours soon. He thought that going on that trip and making connections with colleagues from inside his office and all over the world would get him visibility that would lead to opportunities. His Manager Jennifer thought that was a great idea. Plus, Johnny X had never been to Hawaii before, so he thought that it would be fun anyway.

Johnny X got on the plane to fly out from New York. He saw people from his office on the flight. He was coincidentally assigned a seat next to a guy named Ernest Wheeler, who was the senior account manager on a huge government contract within the firm. Johnny X was on the right next to the window, Ernest was in the middle, and another colleague, a woman named Alecia, sat to the left of Ernest. Johnny X saw this as an opportunity to re-introduce himself to Ernest and chit-chat a little since they had a long flight ahead. However, unbeknownst to Johnny X, Ernest was more interested in talking to Alecia all the way to Hawaii.

"Hi, Mr. Wheeler, I'm Johnny X from Marketing. I'm a junior associate at the firm," Johnny X said with confidence and a big smile.

Ernest grinned and replied, "Cool, nice to meet you. I hope you're looking forward to the summit." Before Johnny X could respond, Ernest got back into his conversation with Alecia.

Feeling slightly played, Johnny X eavesdropped a little bit on their conversation. They talked about an incident that happened with the L.A. basketball team about a week ago. Apparently, Alecia was from Los Angeles and followed them religiously. So Johnny X chimed in and spilled everything he knew about the L.A. team and what was going on with the star of the team at the time.

Fully engaged in the topic, Alecia unbuckled her seat belt so she could turn into the row to talk with Johnny X easier. Ernest became silent and visibly irritated. Johnny X didn't know if it was because he had unintentionally hijacked the conversation, or if Ernest felt that his play on Alecia had slipped away. Nevertheless, Johnny X kept talking and Alecia kept listening.

Johnny X noticed his frustration growing and tried to include Ernest back into the conversation, but Ernest wasn't interested in talking anymore. Johnny X was connecting with the wrong person for his intended mission. Turns out that Alecia was only an entry level associate, and Ernest was one of the project managers she worked for. Johnny X still talked to her the whole flight over, while Ernest chucked a cup of Bourbon and fell asleep between them. So while Johnny X was entertained all the way to the islands, he didn't get to make the key business connection he was hoping for.

When they landed in Hawaii, Ernest was visibly bothered that Johnny X had basically stolen the interest of the young lady. He decided that when they got back to New York, Johnny X would not be added the project he was coincidentally set to work on because Alecia was already working on it as well. Ernest saw a romance brewing in Alecia and Johnny X's eyes, so he wanted to separate them. Johnny X really didn't care about sparking a romance with his colleague, but he did care about finding new work. However, his talkative personality and charm had gotten him in trouble and won him an admirer at the same time. Johnny X had broken all of the social event conversation rules because he lacked the awareness of what was really going on in the situation. Johnny X and Alecia still became great friends/colleagues, and fortunately for him, he was placed on another big project to maintain his billable hours.

Electronic Communications

In this new corporate environment, electronic communication has become very critical communication vehicles. They can sometimes make or break your careers with the ability to timestamp correspondence and also be used as evidence in flawed communications. Just as you are careful with your face-to-face communication, you have to be even more focused when it comes to dealing with email and social media.

The mistakes made in this space live forever and the other downside is that the context is often lost in messages. Age, gender, nationality, and even office terminology play a major role in how electronic communications can be misconstrued. While you cannot control everything regarding your electronic communications, you can make sure that you are doing all you can on your end.

Social media. Social media has made the world a much smaller place—and a more dangerous one for people who like to change their personas based on their audience. There are so many social media sites that people use for both work and pleasure, that there's too many to go through. The lines between your social life and professional life used to be compartmentalized where you were able to separate your friends from your colleagues, your family from your boss, or your pastor from your fraternity brothers.

We all have that one colleague that is a model citizen at work and a miscreant in the street after hours. A co-worker of mine was the most intelligent, thoughtful, professional woman that I had ever worked with. Her name was Lisa. She was an HR generalist and she was definitely a stickler for law and order. She was so stern, that people wouldn't even joke around her in the office. People would tighten up in the hopes that the "HR Sheriff" wouldn't take them down for a misdemeanor.

One year a popular sorority held their annual conference in our city. We all knew that Lisa was a member of this particular sorority, but the videos of her that popped up on YouTube from a few of their parties changed our opinion of her forever. She danced drunk in skimpy clothing and carried on like she didn't work as a human resources professional. Co-workers saw a lot of the wild photos on Instagram and shared them in the office. This caused people in the office to take a more detailed look at what Lisa was doing on her social media sites.

After the fun weekend, Lisa returned to work the next week cracking the whip as usual. Coincidentally, she wrote up one of the female employees from the sales team for wearing inappropriate clothing to work. She retorted to Lisa by showing her a screenshot of what she wore over the weekend. Lisa was embarrassed and livid at the same time. She didn't know how the young lady got those photos, and was beside herself that she had used them as ammunition at work. The "Work Lisa" was much different than the "Weekend Lisa."

You would expect people to be looser and relaxed with their friends, but you don't expect to see the extremes in behavior to have such a negative impact on people's overall reputation. A lot of people don't believe in letting what's private stay private anymore. Most people contend that if it's out on social media for consumption, they can take it into consideration when formulating an opinion of you. Lisa's reputation took a huge hit and she was never promoted beyond generalist. She eventually went to another company.

Social media has fused these worlds of personal and professional lives together in a way that people never have in the history of mankind. You now have that crazy uncle who just started Killing Season Records—shouting you out on LinkedIn—and asking you to share his new mixtape URL with your professional network. Not cool. And so not professional.

Nowadays, when a potential employer or current employer want to know more about you as a person, they can just venture out to Facebook, Twitter, Instagram, LinkedIn, or YouTube, and find out almost anything about you. Who you are affiliated with on social media, how you represent yourself, and the images that you allow of yourself are all reflections of you. Whether or not they're accurate, fair, or taken in the right context, doesn't matter. People will use these sources to judge you, analyze your personality, and your belief system.

We have often seen celebrities go on a Twitter rant about themselves or political issues only to be crucified by the court of public opinion soon afterwards. People have been sued, lost jobs, and even arrested/convicted for things that they have posted on social media.

There are a couple of ways to protect yourself from this. Of course, the first way is to not post content on social media that you don't want everyone to see. Secondly, if you cannot resist the temptation of sharing your life with the world, change your settings to private and only allow your real friends access to your information.

If you have a business profile on social media, there are a few actions that would be very valuable for you to avoid:

1. Do not add your personal friends/relatives to your business social media sites, unless it's for business purposes. You want to minimize the business and personal communication overlaps.

2. Do not have a personal account on the same platform as your business account.

3. Do not connect with your job or boss on social media. (Unless you have to.)

Emails. Emails are the transcripts of your professional life. Important messages, requests, and responses from your manager and colleagues hang in the balance. They exist forever in an Outlook folder or server somewhere in Utah. As you may have seen in politics, emails can come back to haunt you on a future endeavor or actually save you from condemnation. That's why it's important to really think about what you are emailing to people because you never know when your emails/texts will re-surface.

Set up an email repository. One of the most important ways that I handle email messages that I receive is that I organize them. At the beginning of every fiscal year, I create a set of fiscal year (FY) folders and code them by categories, such as by organization and by person. I also create a "props" folder that includes all the positive feedback that I receive. I then create a second folder in my hard drive to save all the attachments, graphics, and other documents that I receive into a main folder with three sub-area folders for each type of item.

It's really good to have your information organized in a way that makes it easy to pull the documents that you need when you need them. You should be very coy about the fact that you save everything because people will be reluctant to email you. Additionally, people may come to you as a resource to borrow your content to possibly cause harm to yourself or others. You don't want to be known as the office snitch that has handed over incriminating documents.

For your G-14 classified materials, you can store copies of your emails on a thumb drive, or bcc your personal email when appropriate, and when you're legally able to do so. You never know when there is going to be a system crash or your computer gets destroyed.

When you send emails, always remember that emails are never truly deleted. They live on a server somewhere forever. Unless you have your own server like the former Secretary of State, someone within your company can access your emails, no matter how old they are. Once you write something down and send it, understand that it can come back to bite you.

Remember that the game is on at all times, including the moments that you write/type your words. That's why before you send an email out to anyone, you should have a sober mind. You should never write an email while you are emotional. Don't ever send angry emails or IM posts to anyone. Don't throw people under the bus in emails either. People will forward your emails to friends, enemies, and your boss to make you look bad at the worst time. So before you respond to an issue or that person that really gets on your nerves, relax. Be certain to calm down and make sure that your message is based purely off of the importance of the business need.

Before you send out *any* email, review, review, and review. Make sure you review your email like it's your final exam to graduate from your toughest college English course. Poor writing skills are shotgun wounds to your professional brand. Spelling and grammatical errors lead people to believe that you are not very smart and that you may possibly be lazy. When in doubt about your skills, find one of the online editing sites to review the email for you as a second set of eyes. Another good idea is to send a test email to yourself to make sure the formatting is good as well.

When sending emails to senior managers, the tone of your messages should always come with deference to management with a positive solutions-oriented tone. You want them to see you as a person who has the work at hand under control with great energy and bright ideas. This not only improves your brand with upper-management, but it also increases the chance that they will hear you out when you write messages or share new ideas with them.

When you're sending emails to your team or colleagues, you should exude a tone of strength and leadership. Don't be humorous in emails because jokes are often taken out of context when written down. Be straight to the point and always thank people for their assistance. Be clear about deadlines and always ask for feedback so that people will see that you're open to discussion when necessary.

When sending emails to an enemy, make sure that you take all of the same actions that you would with your team and other colleagues, but remember that known enemies are always attempting to take you down a notch. They are usually baiting you into a harsh response or will be vague enough to absolve themselves of blame if something goes wrong. You have to remember that enemies are very strategic when it comes to writing email messages. Reiterate what the requests are and force them to spell out expectations to cover yourself on the back-end.

Using the internet. The internet has become a very important resource in our lives. Most people get their news, entertainment, and other important information from the web, such as sports and celebrity gossip. Social media, of course, is its own animal unto itself. Not only have we managed to "outsource" memorized data to Google, web browsing has become a favorite pastime for slackers throughout the world. Unfortunately, this is detrimental to anyone who's required to work on a computer all day.

Nevertheless, in all honesty, no one sits in front of a computer pressing buttons for several hours in a row. There are pockets of time when people read a document, talk to a co-worker/customer, or just stare off into space.

With the blurred line between work-life balance, many people double-dip at work by taking care of personal tasks throughout the day on their work PCs. Paying a bill here and there falls under this category, but is lightweight compared to some people that not only shop for Christmas gifts online, but even check their dating profiles and apply for jobs with other companies. It's strongly encouraged to not use your work computer for these matters.

Some companies have a relaxed policy on internet browsing, but you have to remember that you are on at all times. Someone, somewhere is watching, and everything is recorded. You don't want to get caught surfing the web only to find out that you have violated some archaic policy you didn't know existed.

Risky web surfing could result in a virus on your PC/laptop, or even worse, a breach to your company's network. You don't want to be the person to ruin an entire company because you clicked on an ad that said you won ten million dollars.

Johnny X once worked with a young man named Matthew who was always on Facebook on his computer. One day a young lady walked by and saw what she deemed as inappropriate content on his screen. She reported it and he was written up.

Some say, just get a tint screen so people can't pass by and see what you're looking at, right? However, the IT departments and cyber security teams have access to your PCs at all times, even without you knowing. You don't want your management team to know that you're juggling three women on SinglesOnly.com or that you're shopping for human hair in India.

The safe bet is to only use the net when it's appropriate for your work. The risks of not taking this advice can be devastating.

Post-Game Takeaways:

- ✗ With face-to-face meetings, it's important to: be prepared, dress the part, be confident, be positive, and solutions-oriented.

- ✗ With social events, know when to arrive and leave; connect, compliment, and thank the event planner before leaving; don't over-talk; don't change the subject; and don't discuss controversial topics.

- ✗ With electronic communication, which includes social media, emails, and the use of the internet, maintain a barrier between your personal and professional accounts (social media), keep your messages professional, competent, and confident (email), and use your work computer/laptop for work-related purposes only.

*** GAME TIP ***

Surf on your mobile device or pad, not your work computer. Keep your personal business to yourself. Only surf the internet for what you need specifically to do your job. You never know when your records will be pulled and what will be found.

*** GAME TIP ***

When you go to company events, make sure that you take pictures if there is a photographer in the building. Photos with the management team and colleagues at the event have long lasting benefits. (1) They build relationships and team spirit in the office, (2) pictures with managers and senior executives subconsciously places you among leadership and people of importance in people's minds, and (3) it proves you were there and shows you engaged with your colleagues. Pictures are worth a thousand words, and if you use them correctly, they can tell a great story about you to people that don't know you.

*** GAME TIP ***

When trying to solve a problem, you should let the loudest person talk and put their idea out there first. Let the circle digest their complete thought. When they are done, acknowledge their opinion positively, take from it what's good, and then transition the group into what your solution is. The key is to be the calming, resolute voice at the end of the conversation to determine what is important and what the steps are moving forward. If you blurt out your solution to just be heard first, your idea will be likely ignored, or even worse, hijacked by someone who laid back in the cut, slid in from behind, and took your glory. Have people leave the discussion feeling like you saved the day, while appealing to the egos of the subject matter experts.

*** GAME TIP ***

Although you may have protected yourself on social media, chances are a lot of your counterparts haven't. Make sure to still use the social media platforms as a resource to get information about people. Make sure to like posts and pictures from your co-workers when you see them online. Furthermore, make sure to like and comment on their internal social media posts on sites like Yammer. The only exceptions are when the content is religious, political, or sexually explicit.

*** GAME TIP ***

Never send out raggedy rough drafts via email. Although you think you're just sending a mock-up of ideas or a sample Power Point presentation, most people will still judge your abilities and may still hold on to your brain farts and failed attempts to use against you on a later date. Always send drafts out as polished as possible. If you must send something out before it's ready, name the file accordingly as "rough draft," and be as detailed as possible in your email message.

Playbook Notes

CHAPTER 6

SITUATIONAL FOOTBALL IN THE OFFICE

Pre-Game Analysis:

- ✗ Company reorganization.
- ✗ Company mergers.
- ✗ Replacing a manager.
- ✗ Passed up for a job.
- ✗ Someone coming for your job.
- ✗ Civil War in the workplace.
- ✗ Working remotely.
- ✗ How to leave a job.
- ✗ Office Speak.

The premise of situational football is when the coach makes adjustments to his existing strategy based on the current dynamics of what's happening on the field. Great football coaches always emphasize the importance of planning for all possible contingencies in a game. They stress the ability to be flexible in strategizing game plans specific to each team. A coach's ability to prepare their players by keeping them open to any possible situation that can occur during the course of a game is a metaphor for what you need to be able to do in the office.

Just like playing football, the office requires you to not only understand the situation on the ground, but to have a game-plan and be able to call an audible at the line of scrimmage. We are going to discuss a few situations that you may have to deal with at some point in your career.

Company Reorganization

These processes usually involve a company reconstructing their company methodically by organizations, smaller departments, and ultimately staff. In a lot of cases, there are layoffs and title changes for the employees that are fortunate enough to stay. Aside from updating your resume and LinkedIn profile, there is homework you can do in order to survive the corporate shake-up.

First, determine what the company is actually looking to accomplish in the re-org. This will allow you to know where you need to stand when the plates shift, what type of training you may need, or what organization you should align with. You need to align with the leadership team that is part of the reconstruction. Secondly, find out who's staying, who's going, and who's scared to death and not sure. If you are playing the game the right way, some of this news has come through the grapevine to you already. Knowing where the company is going and who's piloting the plane, provides you the best way of figuring out where you need to land.

Johnny X was working as a marketing manager for a Fortune 500 Company for two years when he learned that his organization was being dissolved. The marketing jobs were being eliminated and the work was outsourced to a marketing firm. He got this inside information from the organization's director a month before it was announced. He learned that this organization was looking to increase their headcount around project management.

Fortunately, Johnny X had recently completed his Project Management Professional (PMP) certification, and reached out to the Business Management Office to express interest in working for this group. The BMO was already impressed with his work, and he successfully transferred into a project manager position, saving himself from the fate of his marketing colleagues. He lived to fight another day.

These types of moves must be precise and calculated, but they require that you are prepared, have your ears to the streets, and are not sharing your intelligence with your colleagues.

Mergers

Mergers are all about who's in charge. Knowing who holds the keys in these types of situations are paramount to your survival. Often the larger company that is coming in usually has the spoils, and brings in their people to conquer the redundant roles within the newly merged company. This leaves the people in the smaller company on the outside looking in or in a subordinate role after taking a demotion.

In the classic movie *Boomerang*, Eddie Murphy played Marcus Graham, the lead character who was a marketing manager for a company called Chantress that was being acquired by cosmetics corporate giant Lady Eloise. Marcus vied to be Director of Marketing. In order to make sure his name was on the top of the list, he allowed himself to be seduced by the face of the company—Lady Eloise herself. Unbeknownst to him, Lady Eloise hadn't lead the company in over a decade and had no power. In fact, it was incoming Executive Jacqueline Broyer (Robin Givens) that took the lead as head of marketing for the new company. Marcus didn't do his homework.

Aside from the fact that it's ethical in the real world, on its face it's still a calculated miscue. Mergers almost always mean that duplicate positions will face cuts from the mother company that is taking over.

Marcus wanted to hedge his bets to be a shoe-in for the leadership role. He had a good strategy (minus the seduction part) in connecting with the presumed most senior person that had influence over designating positions. However, he didn't confirm that his mark was the correct one.

During company mergers, you should not only update your resumes and LinkedIn profile, but you should do your homework to find out who the influencers are and who will be in charge. If you can contact them, and you realize that you can't fairly compete for the role, you may want to befriend them to figure out how, at the very least, you can stay on staff. Sometimes you have to lose to win in order to fight another day.

Replacing a Manager

When a manager leaves the company, people may act like they are sad to see them go, but the reality is that it's an opportunity for almost every person on the team. So in a lot of instances, the people are happy, but no one wants to outwardly admit that they are gunning for the number one spot. Once the decision is made by upper management to fill the position, the gloves come off of everyone. Friends become foes, and the closest colleagues will stab each other in the back to advance themselves.

You need to first decide if you actually want the job. Once you acknowledge that you do, you need to go all out. You need to find out what the hiring manager is looking for to fill the position. Secondly, you need to seek out the competition. Don't let your co-workers know you're interested. The only people you should let in on the plan are the managers who can/will give you a reference.

You should also do a little reconnaissance work on the job and the team that the previous manager was in charge of. This will surely help you in the interview, but can possibly create advocates on the front line as well.

Someone Coming After your Job

This is a code red situation; when someone not only attempts to advance ahead of you, but they aim for the very spot you're standing in. The gloves have to come off in this scenario, but not before you do your reconnaissance work. You need to know not only who's coming, but what the plan is. Like the famous song by the O'Jays says, "They smile in your face, all the time they want to take your place. The backstabbers… baaaack stabbers!"[11]

Often people miss the signs of these Judas operations because it happens so covertly. Some people are so positive and optimistic, that they don't believe that it can happen to them. Starting quarterbacks are almost never best friends with their backups. They can play nice in front of the cameras or for the players and coaches on the team, but in reality, the starting quarterback knows the backup wants to replace him. See Green Bay…

Once you sniff out the backstabber, you must work on your defense. Your defense starts with covering yourself on all fronts. Any good work that you are doing and projects that you are required to deliver need to be done correctly and on time. Make sure that you're creating an email paper-trail for everything. Also, make sure you are not drawn into any situations where you are provoked to be unprofessional. Many of your adversaries will try to sabotage you in front of your boss or send you passive aggressive emails to make you react.

Never get pulled into mudslinging—especially online. All electronic messages last forever, and even the smoothest comeback can be taken out of context. You never know who's working with them on the inside. They could be setting you up for the fall and baiting you with frivolous accusations. Once people see your angry side, it's impossible to put that image out of their mind.

Johnny X was part of a Breast Cancer Awareness campaign for over five years as the program manager and the manager of Marketing and Communications. Everyone thought very highly of Johnny X's campaign, as he had been continuously increasing participation and funds raised for the cause. Not only was this program one of the largest within the company, it led to numerous project management opportunities when Breast Cancer Awareness Month was over. It made Johnny X a rock star and showcased his skills throughout the organization on all levels of management. Other people on the team knew that as well.

Johnny X had a colleague named Gavin, who was a project manager that Johnny X would use to manage a task within the project. Gavin was incredibility jealous of Johnny X and thought that if he could out-shine him or look superior to him, he could steal the job, get all the glory, and get the opportunities for himself. So at every chance, Gavin tried to undermine Johnny X to make him look bad. Gavin scheduled side meetings with senior management to pitch his ideas and build a sub-group within the project team. Johnny X was informed while on his lunch break one Monday afternoon by one of his other colleagues that Gavin was sabotaging him. Johnny X was upset, and it also confirmed what he was already thinking. His "spidey senses" always tingled when Gavin was around. Additionally, he noted some questionable comments that he recalled Gavin making on the conference calls.

On the streets or the basketball court, for example, if someone is hating on you, you're supposed to deal with the issue head on. Verbal confrontations are almost a certainty in these situations, followed by a one-on-one game or a fist fight.

However, in the office, optics are everything, and no one wants to catch an assault charge. You must remember that two rules of the game are at play here: (1) you are on at all times. You do not want to come out of your professional brand and do a "when keeping it real goes wrong" on the perpetrator, which would ruin your career, and (2) in a conflict, you want to flush out the enemy as far out in the light as possible. This is business. Although it makes you angry, do not let anyone provoke you to an emotional response.

That is exactly what Johnny X did. He reached out to his colleague Tia that was part of the project, but was identified as part of his scout team. While on a lunch break, Johnny X casually mentioned that he may be working on a new project and would like Tia to help him with it once it kicks-off. He complimented her abilities with metrics and reporting, and went on about how valuable she would be to him going forward. Tia was flattered, of course, and became very relaxed. Johnny X stood up from the table, and casually said that if any new details come out of the sub-committee with Gavin, to let him know. He insisted that he could definitely use some of those ideas as well. Tia looked puzzled, but thought that Johnny X must know about Gavin's meeting. She agreed to send Johnny X a copy of the meeting notes. Johnny X had everything in place. Tia felt so empowered and excited about the future opportunity that Johnny X had presented, she began to provide him with all types of information that Gavin was doing behind his back. Johnny X worked covertly one step ahead of Gavin. For example, Johnny X took the meeting minutes from the sub-committee meetings and used the information to his advantage. When Gavin went to management and other team members with complaints and his plans for the project, Johnny X pointed out the flaws of the plans. He created even better solutions that were already budgeted and vetted by the necessary departments.

Over time, it began to look like Gavin was disgruntled, bitter, and full of bad, half-baked ideas. Johnny X appeared to be the diligent worker, always thinking about solutions, and saving the day. Johnny X had the ear and trust of upper management, communicated with them regularly about the projects he was working on, and shared with them the success he was having. With every win for Johnny X, Gavin became more frustrated and more desperate to change the tide. He got so desperate that he got sloppy. It eventually became very obvious that Gavin was hating on Johnny X. Many started to notice the negative energy Gavin was giving off. Johnny X was at war, but his demeanor never changed.

It all came to a head when the company decided to split. The company had to decide who to move over and who to keep. Johnny X was such a positive and productive part of the team, management never dreamed of getting rid of him. Unfortunately for Gavin, the General Manager had seen enough; Gavin was given to the new company, along with 20 other employees. Gavin's back-door dealing really bothered management. The GM shared this with Johnny X, along with how he was really impressed with how professional Johnny X had handled the situation. There were no huge blow-ups, incidents, or complaints filed to the GM. Johnny X's wartime strategy went completely unnoticed by nearly everyone, and most importantly, by Gavin.

Someone can come after your position at any time. Some adversaries don't have any standards as to how low they would go to take you out. Once you find out you are a target, it's war time.

When Dealing with Someone Coming for You

Don't be emotional. Never deal with this type of situation when emotions are in the way. Make sure you elect to deal with a person about this matter when it's strictly X's & O's about business. It obviously feels personal when someone is gunning for your position—especially if you could be out of a job. However, the key to winning this war is knowing how to maneuver in Corporate America.

As the famous quote from Jimmy (Tom Hanks) in the movie *A League of their Own* goes, "There's no crying in baseball."[12]

Likewise, there's no crying in the office. You have to use policy within the confines of the job, and use more determined methods in the cloak of darkness.

Vet electronic communications. Don't send electronic communications about the matter unless it's been vetted. Never send angry emails, texts, or voicemails. Remember that this information will be used against you later as receipts of your bad/unprofessional behavior. Only send messages when you are certain that they are professional, have the right tone, and would not be viewed as offensive by your manager or human resources. If you must send out email messages regarding a serious situation, make sure you copy the correct people and properly title the subject lines for later retrieval.

Avoid regrets. Don't say something in front of people that you will regret later. Whether you are on a conference call, in the conference room, at lunch, or even in the restroom, do not threaten or argue with anyone in front of other people. You never know who's for or against you, and you never know how people will interpret your actions. Two people can see the same event and tell a different story.

Win the optics of the argument. Guess what, there are times when you're wrong in a situation and you won't be able to wiggle yourself out. However, this doesn't mean you can't capitalize off of it. Most people who try to prove you wrong in front of others are doing it to elevate themselves and to make you look bad. The best way to make lemonade out of the lemons in these situations is to take control and steal the thunder of the person who's trying to embarrass you.

First, admit fault and take responsibility before they drop the so-called bomb-shell on you. Steal the power of the mic drop from them, while also showing accountability, which is a great attribute for leaders to have. Secondly, transition them into an alternative or solution to the issue at hand. Finally, yield the floor to your oppressor. Make it awkward for them to come after you now. You've stolen their bullets and handed them a peace treaty. Any aggression they show towards you now makes them look petty and mean.

What to do When Someone Comes after You

Keep quiet. Don't let the other person *know* that you *know* that they are coming for you. People are a little sloppier when they don't think you're watching. They will be more willing to risk building alliances against you behind your back. Do your own research on the person. Find out their strengths, weaknesses, habits, and connections. Never tell anyone you know there's a mouse in the house. You will be able to use all of this to your advantage. Knowledge is truly power in this situation. Move in a way that doesn't allow your scout team to know that you are coming for them either. You never know who's working for the other side. Always meet and greet with a smile and a sense of confidence.

Get one step ahead of the enemy. Find out what they actually want to get from you or cause you to do. Insulate yourself in plain sight with the cloak of transparency, niceness, and documentation. When someone is trying to sabotage you, beat them to the punch with documentation of critical things like approvals, rejections, and feedback from the team. Send all receipts and vouchers. Stay on your toes with research and existing information about your work load. Take nothing for granted. People will turn on you in a second if they doubt your skills or abilities in comparison to the competition.

A quarterback hates getting hurt and having to share snaps with the starting offense with the backup who's been studying the schedule and playbook more than he has all season. Not only that, he's been studying the QB too. In some cases, you have to be patient. Sometimes these scenarios play out over time. Start out your defense in a zone package. This means you have to protect your areas and have a safety (Plan "B") so you won't get beat deep or defeated by a long shot attack. You want to know what your enemy's tendencies are. These are easy to exploit and use against the person. It also may be a great idea just to find out who his existing enemies are. They may have two war fronts going on at one time. This is perfect for you. Let the other front deliver wounds and drop bombs on them. These scars and casualties build up and make it easier for you to win.

Pre-discuss details with allies. Make sure that you pre-discuss some of the details with superior participants in your meetings so that you will have allies on the call with you. People like to hear information regurgitated to them that they already agree with. Get pre-meeting buy-in from the decision makers, then present it to the group. Have your enemy set themselves up to be in conflict with you and the head managers. This is like laying down land mines for your enemy to step on during war. Having allies, especially superiors, are always great to have.

Always stay calm. Remember that you are always on, and you don't want your enemy's sarcasm or ambush tactics to throw you off your game. This is just like in football when the blitz is coming; always have a check down pass or hot route to throw to so that you can move the chains. For example, let's say you're in a meeting discussing a project and a colleague has a question for you that is off topic. One of the easiest ways to handle this is to take the question with grace, and let the person know that you can take it "offline," or at some other time. That means it's not going to be discussed now because it would take you off the current topic. This response can have other meanings as well, but we'll get into this phrase later.

Jay Z has a bar from his song the "Takeover" that says, "A wise man told me don't argue with fools because people from a distance can't tell who is who."[13]

You don't want to be viewed as "the angry guy," "the crazy lady," or "the weirdo" in the office.

Make sure people know you won. After a battle like this goes down, if people find out about it (and they will), make sure they know you won the war. Not in a way that makes you look petty or evil, but delicately enough to know that you professionally endured it. You don't want them to see you as a bully, but rather as someone who is smart, professional, and connected. This battle tested confidence will win you fans and teach people not to come after you.

Let's look at an example. When a person comes home from prison, the guys in the neighborhood treat the newly-released convict like a hero. It's not because prison is a great place; it's what prison represents in its rawest form in the hood. He's been battle tested and proven, so no other gangster in the hood will question his toughness, nor do they want to have to be measured against him. He is either hailed with acceptance, or people run to get out of his way.

It's the same way in the office. If you make it through situations where your job is threatened or colleagues are conspiring to ruin your reputation, people will make sure to not cross you. You will also gain loyalty from places you never expected to.

Passed up for a Job

Being passed over for a position is one of the most disappointing experiences that can happen to you in a company next to being fired. Have you ever applied for a job internally, talked to the hiring manager, met all the qualifications, have been working in that area or with the team this position will support, got a recommendation letter from a senior manager, saved a choking co-worker in the breakroom, and still didn't get the job? It happens more than you think, and it's one of the leading causes of dissension in the office and the reason employees seek opportunities elsewhere.

Now, the fact remains, there are times when someone else is better than you for a job. It happens, and in that regard, you just have to step up your game. Get some additional training, find a mentor, or do more mock interviews.

There are instances where you have done or said something unbeknownst to you that got back to the hiring manager that got you disqualified. This is why you shouldn't talk to your co-workers about your career ambitions. You never know whose selling you out behind the scenes or paving a way for themselves. Sometimes you get clear indications that politics are at play.

Johnny X was a contractor for a large technology company and had ambitions of becoming a full time employee. As his contract was coming to an end, he was encouraged by his then manager to apply for a permanent marketing position in his area of expertise that had become available. Johnny X applied for the job, and in a matter of days, he was on the phone with the hiring manager for a phone interview. After a great interview, they flew him out to the company headquarters for an in-person interview. Johnny X was feeling great about his chances to land this job. After all, he had a master's degree, 10 years of experience instead of the 5-year required minimum, and he had a working relationship within the department already. His current manager also put in a really good plug for him when the hiring manager called her for a reference.

When Johnny X arrived into town, the face-to-face interview was better than the phone interview. The hiring manager loved him. He introduced Johnny X to all of the people in headquarters. He walked him around the building to see the operation in greater detail. He was even asked about a start date.

Johnny X had a great flight home, and was eagerly awaiting for an offer letter via email. Unfortunately, after a few days, the email didn't come. Johnny X sent a thank you email to the recruiter and hiring manager to check in and they didn't respond at all. Finally, after about two weeks, Johnny X got in touch with the recruiter via instant message. She informed him that he did not get the job. When he asked why, she said that they wanted someone located at headquarters. Before Johnny X could get another word in, she cut him off, said that she was in a hurry for a meeting, and logged out of IM. He never heard back from the hiring manager either. He had just flown Johnny X across the country for an interview and paraded him around the entire senior staff, but at this point, acted like he didn't even know him.

In the meantime, Johnny X luckily extended his contract for an additional six months, but as faith would have it, he was assigned to work on a big contract with the new marketing manager that had the job that he thought was supposed to be his. He sent the young lady an email to set up a conference call, but she told him that they could meet in person.

Johnny X was confused because he thought the recruiter said that they wanted a person who worked in the headquarters area, which was five states away. She stood up at her cubicle and waved to Johnny X to come over to her cubed workspace for an impromptu meeting.

Johnny X was shocked, but he went over to talk. He felt like Miss Columbia in the 2015 Miss Universe Pageant when the host announced her as the winner by accident only to take the crown off her head to give it to Ms. Philippines.

Her name was Cassie and she seemed nice, but Johnny X was salty because she had *his* job. Before they got down to business, Johnny X tried to make small talk. He snuck in a question to her about when she applied and interviewed for the job. Her response made him want to jump out of the window. She told him that she never even applied or interviewed for the job. The hiring manager was her former boss and he told her a month ago that he had a new job for her. She went on to explain that she really didn't want the job because she was enjoying being a stay-at-home mom. She had just decided at the last minute to take the job. She told Johnny X that he was put on the project to teach her how to do the work and to help her write the marketing plan. She was actually an accountant.

As cold as it sounds, this happens often to people in the workplace. It especially happens to minorities and women, according to numerous studies that have been done. People give you a plethora of weak excuses to justify their bias and make you feel good enough to return to doing your old job. There are common reasons candidates are given when skipped over for a less talented and/or experienced person.

Common Reasons to be Skipped Over for a Less Talented Person

1. "We went with an external candidate because we wanted some fresh perspective."

2. "We hired a person with senior level experience from another department."

3. "We have another opportunity coming up that will be a better fit for you."

4. "We wanted a person located in a specific region."

5. "We didn't know you were interested in this area."

6. "This position was created for a specific person, but we had to interview people to be in compliance with our labor laws and HR policies."

In reality, the boss hired their son-in-law, or they hired a person they were attracted to, or in some cases of insecurity, they thought you were a threat to them, and therefore chose *not* to hire you.

There's an old saying that goes, "it's not what you know, it's who you know!" If you're passed up for a position by a person the management team already identified, there's nothing much you can do about their decision. What you can control is how you prepare yourself for that next opportunity. Do whatever you can to eliminate the excuses as to why you were skipped over.

Steps to Overcome Competition Next Time

1. Make sure your manager, not your colleagues, know what your career path is. Document it in your performance review; develop goals and objectives to work towards achieving them.

2. Get whichever additional certifications you need to get the edge; technical, administrative, project management, or whichever certification the new job requires. Note, in most cases, your company will pay for these certifications.

3. Participate in sub-committee programs at work to showcase your talents. Even if you don't want to go to the pot luck or happy hour... *just go.*

4. Keep your ear to the streets to get a jump on the competition. Learn everything you can on the ground before you reach out to the hiring manager. See if you can learn if management already has a candidate identified.

5. Ask for feedback on your interview. Find out what you need to work on. Do mock interviews to sharpen your skills, improve your body language, and your ability to

think of and explain work examples.

6. Build your advocate list of senior management. Get people with power to co-sign you once you're in the interview process.

Take their ability to make excuses about why they aren't awarding you with what you have earned and put those excuses to rest. Force them to expose their bias and hypocrisy if they exist. If you think you're being discriminated against and you're not willing to go back to the drawing board, do what you feel is necessary from a legal perspective or within the guidelines of your company's Human Resources policy. However, you should be careful; make sure your complaint is legit. Filing grievances and complaints are like having challenge flags in the NFL; you can only throw it twice. You don't want your reputation to be marred by constant complaints when things don't go your way. Two times is a coincidence, three times is a pattern.

Losing a Beloved Colleague

Losing a loved one in any walk of life is a sad occasion, especially if you were close to them. You send condolences to the family—typically with a group donation for flowers and a card that everyone signs. There is also an email that goes out to the office, expressing sadness for the person lost and everyone shares their warm sentiments and stories about their fallen colleague.

About a week or so later, the solemn mood subsides and reality sets in. Depending on the fallen person's position, it may start sooner rather than later, but what people in the office really want to know is who's taking the spot of the person who died. Most people don't want to appear to be a cold-hearted bastard, but in all seriousness, some people really want that job.

Instead of appearing to be an insensitive person, you can still vie for the job while being helpful. The easiest way to do it is to start by asking his/her manager if you can take over the work of the person who died. Let them know that you're a stop-gap and are there to help the situation. On one hand you're taking on extra work, but it's an investment in your future. By helping the manager, you show your boss that you are willing to be a team player and you're auditioning for the job. Either way, it's a win/win for you.

Honor your fallen co-worker in the office by doing something sentimental that people will appreciate. Any small gesture like an office procedure or desk fixture would be sufficient. You want to show compassion that allows people to feel like you appreciated the person who died, while at the same time, you avoid appearing as if all you want is the come up.

Johnny X worked at a company where a guy died from a heart attack. He was one of the senior account managers in their department. Johnny X collected money from the employees in the department, and with it, bought flowers and a card for the family. He also got a sandwich named after him in the cafeteria. It was a small token, but people rallied around Johnny X for helping the office get through the loss. People came out of the woodwork inquiring about the job of this deceased man. People even took his equipment off of his desk. His wireless mouse, docking station, umbrella, and even his headset vanished shortly after he passed away. Johnny X and another co-worker were given his accounts to manage in the meantime. The other co-worker was his best friend in the office whom he shared a cubicle with. However, when the smoke cleared, Johnny X was moved into his role and had the full support of management and the deceased man's closest colleagues.

Civil War in the Workplace

What does civil war in the office actually mean? Civil war happens when there are other people in the office fighting for a plethora of reasons. People can fight over a project, budget, a position, or anything. These are the battles that have leaked out in the presence of other people within the office for everyone to see. Two of the major reasons these issues become public are because someone who considers another person a colleague and a friend has shared information with them, or someone is very emotional, and thus becomes sloppy in how they move about the office. Whatever the reason, it is "on and popping" in the workplace, and depending on who it is, people will begin to take sides. In certain cases, members of the management team will begin to take sides as well. You then have a full on civil war that will not end until the strongest faction ends up getting what they want.

How to Survive the Office Civil War

Do not pick a side. If you can help it, be like Switzerland as long as you can. Be neutral. Don't take any position on a fight that does not involve you.

1. **Do *not* divulge information to opposing sides.** The G code (Gangster) is to be followed in Corporate America as well. Don't be a snitch.

2. **Do listen.** Your primary job for self-preservation and triumph out of this situation is to simply listen. Gather as much information as you can about what's going on and what the demands are. Pay attention to the players; see who is doing and saying what. Find out where people's loyalty lies and who the snakes are. Make mental notes to yourself.

3. **Be a problem solver.** If you feel like you have the power and/ or the solution to end the civil war peacefully, then go for it. Everyone loves a war hero and your ability to show your conflict resolution skills will be priceless going forward.

4. **Be a helper.** If you're dragged into war by a friend/ colleague, help them as a wounded backup quarterback. Practice with the scout team offense where you can help your colleague's starting defense without being seen. This simply means to help your friend without leaving a paper trail that will implicate your name. Make sure you offer up just enough to let your people know that you have their back.

5. **Do apply office game knowledge.** If you find yourself in the civil war, it's time to employ everything that you have learned about the office game and play it to the fullest. The key is to survive and to be part of the reconstruction period when the smoke clears.

Working Remotely

The standard workday is now changing for a lot of business professionals. It used to be common for people to wake up, follow their rigorous morning routine, struggle through rush-hour traffic, and make it to work for 9 a.m. sharp to punch a time clock or log into their computer. Their workday would not end until 5 p.m. on the dot, followed by a mad dash back into rush-hour traffic to get home or to pick up the kids. People would have to use vacation and sick leave to run errands and go to doctor's appointments during the workday. However, technology has afforded individuals the opportunity to be more flexible with their time. The ability to work remotely or via smartphone has opened up a whole new world of convenience and potential career ending traps for today's business professional.

Working remotely has its advantages if you can manage it correctly. You not only have to manage the workload, but you have to be available for meetings and make sure the home office optics don't cast you in a negative light. If your boss can't trust you to work from home, they can't trust you at all. Make sure, beyond a shadow of a doubt that they believe in your abilities to be productive, creative, and to be able to react promptly and effectively to emergency situations.

Make sure that you have everything you need to do your job outside of the office. Having a virtual private network (VPN) set up is paramount. If you don't have it, you may have to download needed documents off of the intranet in advance. Make sure you have access to the sites you need, email, and instant message.

If you can help it, do not work remotely when a project is due that you need to collaborate on or if senior management is in the building that day. You definitely don't want the vice president of your organization to come by and see your desk empty, so you must be aware of what's happening in your building.

Make sure that you can access your instant messenger at all times. Most managers will use your IM login to see if you are online. Most indicators have a red or green light display next to your photo. It's the first place they will check on you by sending a quick message to see if you will respond and how long it will take you to do so. There are great workarounds for this. One is to get the IM platform on your mobile device as well, so if you're in the car, in the bathroom, or on your lunch break, you are still available virtually. You should *always* be ethical—even when no one is watching. Run your errands on honest breaks, but still be available and connected to your team.

Once you have everything you need to functionally do your job, you need to refer back to Chapter 5 on "Communications" and multiply the actions three times. You will need to create a super virtual image to make sure your presence is felt when you are not in the office. Out of sight, out of mind is usually the mindset in the corporate setting. At every given moment, you must show yourself in a great light and remind people of your importance and engagement level.

Be sure that all your inter-office online profiles have an image—especially an image of you smiling. When people see your face on a Skype call, they should see a positive image of you.

It's always good to switch your photo around every few months. Employees will see you as an active member of the staff. Additionally, when you're joining a conference call, be the first one. The last thing that you want to do is join the call late when people are aware that you are working from home. You will look like you were doing laundry or washing your car while wearing a headset.

Don't be the person that dishonestly accuses Skype of "acting up today" or lying that your phone was on mute. Logging on the phone early usually gives you a few minutes with the host of the call, which will not only show them that you manage working remote responsibly, but you get some one-on-one time with the host or other senior staff on the call.

Make sure you post content on the internal social media pages and intranet articles. This will show that you're engaged, but it will also time-stamp your activities online.

Be more flexible when it comes to meetings outside of your normal working hours. Here is the part of the give-and-take where you will have to focus on the giving part. Within this global economy, you have to work with colleagues and clients from around the world at some point. Everything won't happen within the convenient timeframe of your 9 a.m. – 5 p.m. workday. Being available early in the morning or later in the afternoon will show your boss that there is an advantage to you working at home. You're able to take meetings during a time that you would be in rush-hour traffic.

Once you have solidified yourself as a fully engaged and virtual version of yourself, you are now safe to move about the cabin. You will be able to enjoy the flexibility of being a true remote worker. It's like being a great football player in the prime of your career. Your coaches know that you are a championship caliber player, so you get the benefit of the doubt when you miss practice or drop a pass in the game. In the office you have successfully built a reputation that allows you to take the foot off the gas when necessary and coast.

Sustaining your Remote Status

The key to maintaining the status quo as a remote employee is to always remember the golden rule: be on at all times! Never take the status for granted and go missing from the scene when it's time to meet. Be available, over-communicate, and create lighthearted social interactions to stay emotionally connected to your colleagues.

Furthermore, you have to remember that some managers or haters will try to make you look bad by checking on you randomly to see if they can catch you slipping. Show them your ability to be consistent and still perform at a high level, if not better, in a home office.

Working virtually is awesome and sometimes necessary, but you still have to provide the human contact experience when you can. The office parties and quarterly meetings are good, but you have to do a little more than make these occasional appearances. Drop into the office on a regular day from time-to-time and work in the main area. Let people see you in the department. Walk down the halls a few times. Most will forget that you're even working remotely, which is exactly what you want. Show your face, give a few high fives, chill out in the break room, and meet the crew for lunch. Show the people who may be bitter that you're working from home that you are still cool and connected to the team members that are stuck in their cubicles.

Finally, as I mentioned before, it's a good idea to change your profile pictures every few months so that co-workers can see you evolve as the weeks, months, and years go by. Do you know someone that has the same Outlook photo from 2005 and they look totally different today?

Working After Hours

So your boss has asked you to work on a project over the weekend and you already have plans. You don't want to seem like you're not being a team player, you don't want your boss to give the assignment to someone else either, but you don't want to ruin your trip to Vegas or your time with the kids at the beach. What do you do?

Taking work assignments after hours is tricky, but there is a simple process and set of best practices to minimize the impact of being bogged down by after hour assignments.

How to Handle After Hour's Responsibilities

1. **Determine urgency and scope of work.** Find out if it's actually a crisis at all. Your boss may actually be panicking about a non-issue.

2. **Negotiate what needs to be done.** If you find out that you have to work, negotiate. This request may be able to be handled before the weekend starts or when you get back. Don't be afraid to push back a little. If you deliver on your promise, your boss will learn to trust you in these situations.

3. **Delegate duties behind the scenes.** Create a shadow sub-committee of people that you know will be able and willing to work on weekends. Contrary to popular belief, there are people who love to work weekends and brown-nosers who would never say no. Use their services.

4. **Set expectations going forward.** No doubt that there will be a major crisis when your services will be needed at a time that directly conflicts with your personal after hour's schedule. After you successfully save the day for your boss, you have to set some ground rules to protect your free time going forward. You don't want weekend work to become a habit. You want to appear available and willing to help, but you also don't want to blur the line between work and life to where it doesn't exist anymore. You work to live, not live to work.

Tips to Maintain Work-Life Balance

1. **Set time boundaries.** Don't complain to your boss, but they need to know that you have obligations and responsibilities to manage during your off time. Work-

life balance is important. Make sure to communicate that whenever you have the opportunities to do so. Embed it in their subconscious mind that you're really not available all the time.

2. **Learn your manager's work style and patterns.** Cut issues off before they happen. Sometimes you have a manager with bad time management skills. Help them manage the tasks that will ultimately affect your workload. Talk to your manager, and if appropriate, their executive administrator to anticipate certain challenges before they arise.

3. **Log out of your email once you leave the office.** Unless you're required to stay online, completely log out of your email if you're not scheduled to work. If you get a text message from your boss, you should respond to the first one, but going forward you should very diplomatically let your boss know that it's more effective for you to receive emails rather than text messages. Unless it's a company phone, set a boundary with your mobile device. Let your colleagues know that email or calling on the phone is the preferred way to contact you. You do not want employee text threads running on your phone through the night and over the weekend.

How to Prepare to Leave a Company

Sometimes you can play the game as good as Michael Jordan played basketball in the 1990s, but still come to the conclusion that it is time to change teams. It can be for a variety of reasons. You could have found another job, you're going to be laid off, or you were moved to a department you can't bear to be in. Maybe you have been moved to a location that's inconvenient to travel to, your schedule has been changed, or you may just be tired of being there. Whatever the reason is, you are ready to go.

Having your reputation intact as best as possible while you're gone is almost just as important as it was when you were there. You never know when/if you're going to need to come back, get a reference, or work under a person that you previously quit working for.

With today's social media, your previous colleagues and managers are a point-and-click away from you, and people are willing to expose your previous transgressions more willingly because they don't have to face you after they do it. They can ruin your next opportunity behind the comforts of a keyboard. This is part of the reason that you need to know how to leave a company with your integrity intact.

Have a plan. This is the first step. Do not get bad news from your current employer and move impulsively based on your emotions. You need months to remember that this is going to be a decision that follows you throughout your professional career. You may need these folks for a reference, and even worse, it may take you a couple of months or even a year before you find a new job in your field. If you can, please do not leave your current job unless you have a new one. Begin your plan with a timeline. Start with your next job or career move on the far right side of the line, including the start date. Then work backwards from that date to figure out all the tasks that you need to take care of leading to that date.

Use the divorce tactic. If you don't have a plan, you need to start creating one as soon as you have the itch to go elsewhere. It's sort of like when people are thinking about divorcing their spouses. You know how the divorce plan works:

- ✗ Get your paperwork in order.
- ✗ Start building a new social network.
- ✗ Secure a new spot (if you can).
- ✗ Separate finances.
- ✗ Make yourself look more attractive to new prospects.
- ✗ Don't totally destroy your path back to where you came from.

Get your paperwork in order. Update your resume and your LinkedIn profile. Make sure you upload your new resume to all the job finder sites. Next, secure all the documents (legally) that you can use to showcase your work to new employers. You do not want to have to go back to gather these later.

Start building a new social network. You need to audit your existing contact list to make sure you have current contact information on your existing network. Make sure all the email addresses and phone numbers of potential job resources are good. Connect with them on Twitter, LinkedIn, and Facebook.

Afterwards, it's time to add new people to your updated network. Make sure that you are following the places that you are interested in working for on LinkedIn and Twitter at the very least. Every time you apply for a job or receive an email from a staffing agency, see if that person has accounts on these two sites. If they have one, invite them to connect or follow them. If they don't have one, at least follow the company they work for.

Note that it's important to post regularly on these social media platforms. You want to post engaging topics and messages that will grab people's attention. You also want to keep up on current events and trends happening in your industry. The more informed and up to date you are, the more people you will appeal to. If you're not the social media butterfly or writing type, just share things that you think are interesting. When people are deciding to connect with you, it will help if you appear to be active.

Secure a new spot (if you can). Even if you are not ready just yet, you should apply for jobs as early and as often as possible. The average timeframe that it takes to find a job making the same amount of money you're currently making is anywhere from three months to one year. Not only do you want to hedge your bets, but you also want to have as much interviewing practice as possible. Just like dating, interviewing is challenging sometimes when you haven't done it in a long time. You want to get your name out there in the industry that you're interested in working in. If you actually get some early offers, you now have an opportunity to control your destiny a little more. You may get your dream job earlier than you thought or you may create a bridge that you can use at another time.

Some people often wait until they are laid off to start looking for a job, but don't realize that it is much harder to get a job when you don't have one. Not sure why this is the case, but it's often been this way in most people's experiences. Like being married, some people say it's because you're more attractive when someone else wants you. It's as if the unemployed person doesn't get the benefit of the doubt as to why they are out of work. If you don't have a job, it's obviously your fault, right? People have lamented that not having a job encourages employers to low-ball you on your job offers because they suspect that you are desperate to work and you surely won't spend two weeks negotiating your salary.

Separate finances. When you are preparing to leave your company, you need to make sure your finances are in order. If you can help it, you don't want to leave any money on the table. This includes bonuses, vacation time, stock options, and 401(k) matches. You need to learn, know, and understand where all your money is and where it is going to go upon your departure.

Consult with Human Resources, the finance department, and whomever else that you would need to speak with to get the most accurate information possible regarding your money. For instance, find out if you get to keep your vacation time and learn the rules about your stock options. You don't want to assume that you're getting some form of compensation and be wrong.

Make yourself look more attractive to new prospects. Just like when a person has finalized their divorce, it's time to revamp your image for your next opportunity. Not only do you want to have a "new attitude" like Patti LaBelle sung in her classic song by the same name, but you have to enhance your digital footprint and update your credentials.[14]

After you get your new haircut/hairstyle and full makeover, take some new professional headshots for all of your social media accounts. Make sure people you want to connect with, including colleagues from your past, see you in a different, polished, and more refreshed light.

Once your image is together, you need to build yourself up on social media, especially on LinkedIn. Your connections should know about all the cool things that you're working on and are a part of. You want to be the person that everyone wants to be around, whether it's working on a project or having a drink. Even your current employers and management may see this and may do more to get you to stay. You have to be your own public relations team to brand yourself as the hardest working and most positive man or woman on the market.

Have all of your certifications and organization memberships updated. Everything that you could use for a future job needs to be current and at your disposal. If your current company offers training certifications or memberships, get them—even if it's something that you don't need right now.

Don't totally destroy your path back to where you came from. If you have to resign, make sure that you extend nothing but love to your employer. Now is not the time to run down your "screw you" list.

Exiting Don'ts

1. **Don't tell everyone that you're leaving before you go.** Once you decide to leave the company, you should not share your plan until you are absolutely 100% okay with people knowing about it. Sometimes if a company finds out that you are planning to leave, they'll get rid of you sooner than you are planning to go. Additionally, you may change your mind about leaving. You don't want to have egg on your face or destroy your manger's confidence in you. If you decide to stay and you've threatened to leave out of the blue, your company may not want to continue to invest in your career. It's like when a disgruntled player requests a trade from his team publicly in the media, but finds out that the franchise is not able to get rid of him just yet. Now he has to play with teammates that know he wants to go. Awkward. If you can help it, you do not want to have to work in an environment where you are public enemy #1. The probability of truly healing the misstep is nearly impossible, and you're more likely to be sabotaged or simply shut out going forward.

2. **Don't say anything bad about anyone or the company on the way out.** When people ask why you're leaving, reiterate how much you love the company and your co-workers. People are looking and listening to everything you do and say. You do not want to have any negative headlines to get back to people. Keep your reputation intact to the end.

3. **Resolve all negative relationships.** Even though you're heading out of the door, this is the perfect time to make amends with anyone that you've had beef with in the workplace. It's good for a couple of reasons. First, it makes it easier to come back to the company. You have no idea who will be in charge of what when you get back. Today's

mid-level analyst is tomorrow's vice president. Secondly, you may need them for references, future collaborations, or expertise.

So many times, an out of work quarterback has been looking for a job and he suddenly finds favor with a team that his old QB coach is currently the head coach of. There once was a Chicago Quarterback, who had arguably fallen off the map as a professional talent, got signed to a one-year, $10 million contract, not because he was still an elite player, but because he was familiar with the coach and his system. Against all the other talent that was available to the coach of the Miami team, he ultimately took who he was comfortable with.

You want to make sure that even on the way out, people are comfortable with you enough to consider having you back if possible. Sometimes you need to forgive and make peace with people that may not deserve it. You never know who you're going to need down the road. You don't want negative energy on you. In a weird twists, former enemies are converted to supporters of you. After all, you're not a threat in the office anymore, and you have earned the respect of some of them to the point where they are willing to support you. Again, as mentioned earlier in this book, this is the exception with enemies.

Additionally, you don't want to have the baggage of failed professional relationships carrying over into your new role. It's like when a person that has been cheated on gets into a new relationship, but struggles with trusting their new partner. To forgive and move on are great moves for you physiologically and professionally.

Timeline acceleration. Finally, if you suspect that the drop is about to come down on you, and you feel like you may not have the time to execute your plan, these steps need to be accelerated. If you don't have a new job and you suspect you're going to be terminated, secure the new job first. The next priority should be securing your finances and compiling your paperwork. You can push off working on your network last because you should be able to still reach the people that you need to after you leave the company.

Office Speak: What it Really Means

Some call French the language of love. Well, Office Speak is the language of corporate catchphrases. It's a mixture of political correctness, passive aggressiveness, and self-aggrandizement. Often in Corporate America, phrases are used by upper management that sound very professional and tempered when you hear them or read them in internal communications throughout your company or organization. What are they really saying?

Sometimes you find yourself confused as to why a colleague stormed out of a room after hearing what you interpreted as a pretty good response to a tough question. It's not until you get the backstory after a situation has exploded, that you begin to understand the loaded commentary you may have witnessed.

In some instances, Corporate Communications departments and Human Resources are more cryptic than the mainstream media when it comes to delivering messages. Understanding these riddles wrapped up in mysteries usually comes with years of experience, but I'm going to provide you with a few of them so that you will know for sure what is happening around you. Of course, there can be an entire book written just to discuss all of these.

24 Examples of Office Phrases

1. "We're going through a transformation." *Translation: A lot of changes can be expected in a company transformation. Whole departments may even get cut and people are most likely losing their jobs. The company strategy is shifting, which can definitely mean a lot of positive changes too.*

2. "We are optimizing/streamlining operations." *Translation: Don't immediately panic and assume that you're losing your job. However, do be aware that significant changes are on their way, particularly in terms of letting employees go who may not be reaching their performance targets.*

3. "Keep me in the loop." *Translation: I am insecure about my position and I need to be needlessly included in on*

as many things as possible, or I need to know what's happening, even though I am not doing any of the work.

4. "We need to move the needle." *Translation: Actually accomplish something—anything, please.*

5. "Use best practices." *Translation: Do the stuff that worked before.*

6. "Check in." *Translation: We need to make sure that you're online or in the office when you say you are.*

7. "You don't have to call, but we can chat on IM." *Translation: I really don't want to talk, just text me.*

8. "Let's table this conversation." *Translation: I don't want to talk about this stuff right now. Never speak of this again.*

9. "I'm just trying to touching base." *Translation: You didn't respond to my last three emails. Where are you?*

10. "Can you provide a 'use case'?" *Translation: I don't really think your idea makes any sense, but maybe you can explain an actual real world application of it that will mean something.*

11. "Show us your value add in the presentation." *Translation: A secret sign to make sure as many people as possible know exactly what good things you've done and what you bring to the company because they haven't been paying attention.*

12. "Does anyone have the bandwidth for this?" *Translation: I'm not interested in doing this and I need to pass this off to someone else or is there any slacker out there willing to do some real work?*

13. "Can I pick your brain for a second?" *Translation: Can you give me an idea because I have no idea of what I am doing?*

14. "What are the lessons learned here?" *Translation: What are the things you messed up on and shouldn't repeat going forward?*

15. "Let's take this offline." *Translation: Let's talk about this away from everyone else because either it's about to get real, or I don't want to be embarrassed about the fact that I don't know what I am doing.*

16. "This needs some wordsmithing." *Translation: This draft is terrible and it needs to be rewritten.*

17. "It is what it is." *Translation: I think I should say something here, but I got nothing. So I am just going to wrap this up.*

18. "Take care of the low-hanging fruit." *Translation: Let's do the easy stuff first!*

19. "Put this on the backburner." *Translation: A certain project or goal is no longer a priority and doesn't need the time, energy, or attention that it once needed.*

20. "This is an evolving situation." *Translation: We really have no idea of what's going on, but we are going to make adjustments as the situation changes to still appear to be right and in control.*

Email messages:

21. "Per my last email/ to reiterate..." *Translation: Like I already stated earlier, and you seem to not understand what I said. You may need to re-read it. (This carries a very passive aggressive tone in an email).*

22. "Moving forward..." *Translation: Don't try me again. From here on out, this is how I'm going to deal with you.*

23. "I've copied <person's name>..." *Translation: So you cannot lie on me later, I am sharing this with management. I am creating a paper trail of evidence in case things go sour.*

24. "Make sure to cc me." *Translation: Do not conduct any business regarding my team or my program without copying me on it. I need to know everything that's going on.*

As you move forward in your career, you will hear things and you will get a feeling of what the undercurrents are behind people's words. Pay attention to their body language, adjust to what's happening around a situation, and apply that when you are reading and interpreting messages. Always feel your way through these situations and remember that your responses will be archived forever. Always be calculated and be 100% sure that you understand the context of what's being said to you. Keep the mental list in your head.

Post-Game Takeaways:

✗ When dealing with difficult situations in the office, such as company reorganization, mergers, replacing a manager, and getting passed over for a job, be sure to be prepared, have back-up plans, listen, and use your scout team to get information that helps position you in a good place.

✗ Take and apply the six provided steps to overcome being passed over for a position in the future.

✗ Understand what an office Civil War is and how to effectively survive one.

✗ Know how to work remotely and still be connected with your team and office.

✗ Know how to please your boss and still maintain a work-life balance with after hour requests.

✗ Know how to effectively and professionally leave a company.

✗ Office Speak: common verbal/written phrases in which to familiarize yourself.

*** GAME TIP ***

Sometimes taking a demotion during a merger isn't always a bad thing. Ego sometimes forces people out the door prematurely when they feel played by the new parent company that only wants their people in leadership roles. Sometimes you have to realize that the goal is to survive and live to earn another paycheck while you figure out your next move. Sometimes you have to sit in the cut and wait for your opportunity to present itself.

*** GAME TIP ***

If someone sends you a long written email detailing an event and attempting to corner you into confession or admitting to doing something, assume it's a ploy to entrap you. *Do not* reply to this email to defend yourself. Set up a face-to-face meeting and talk to the person to find out what's going on. If you are not able to meet face-to-face, get on a call. After you get the details of what's going on, you verbally make your case for or against, and then you send an email back to re-iterate your position. Never submit a written response without talking first, regardless of how egregious or insulting the email message you received. Nine times out of ten, they are documenting this to use against you later.

*** GAME TIP ***

Use your internal network to find out about a manager leaving in advance. By the time the streets find out, the senior leadership has usually identified a person. You want this intelligence on the front end so you can start positioning yourself.

Playbook Notes

CHAPTER 7

THE 10 OFFICE GAME COMMANDMENTS

Pre-Game Analysis:

✗ Learn the 10 fundamental rules to the Office Game.

Just like maintaining a Project Management Professional (PMP) certification, learning the Office Game is an ongoing journey. There are fundamental rules and best practices that will never change. However, there are additional deviations that will evolve as you progress in your career. Understanding the fundamentals is key. Learning how to process situations that you find yourself in while in the workplace is paramount. Each new experience and event that you witness will hopefully add to your cache of lessons learned and best practices. The hope is that you are able to assess the situation and apply the best course of action.

10 Office Game Commandments

1. Thou shall be aware. They are always watching and listening.

2. Thou shall not share new ideas with colleagues. Don't give your talent away.

3. Thou shall not share career goals with peers. People may block/beat you.

4. Thou shall not be transparent. Don't let people see behind your curtain—*ever*!

5. Thou shall listen. Let others complain about things and people.

6. Thou shall not date a colleague. This can cause potential career damage.

7. Thou shall have a Plan B, C, and D. Always be prepared.

8. Thou shall over-dress and then dress it down. Image is important.

9. Thou shall protect oneself. Assume their intent is bad; be okay if it's good.

10. Thou shall be good to everyone. Never throw anyone under the bus.

Thou shall be aware.

As time goes by, people develop what appears on the surface to be strong relationships that transcend the thin and often dotted line between being colleagues and friends. The reality is that although you may enjoy some fun times with your co-workers or you may be able to vent about personal problems to them, the threat of layoffs or the lure of a new position can turn the most loyal co-worker into the competition.

So what you guys go out for lunch. So what you work out at the same gym. So what you share dirty jokes or exchange rumors. When the temperature is turned up, survival instincts kick in and, in most cases, people will do whatever they need to do.

Colleagues are one story, but the next level is an even more slippery slope. Your favorite manager who usually lets you leave a few minutes early or cut corners on a tedious process will let you know at the most inopportune time that they are the boss and you are the employee. Never take this for granted. Whenever you are faced with a situation and the boss is letting his/her figurative hair down, don't break outside of your professional zone. It's okay to be looser or more tolerant of social behavior. If your boss dives off of the hotel balcony into the swimming pool, it's okay to sit poolside and put your feet in the water. However, it's never going to be okay for you to dive in as well.

Johnny X worked in Human Resources with his HR Director Derrick Moore who was a former professional football player. D. Moore, as he was affectionately known by his staff, would always come to the cafeteria, sit with some of the guys in the office, and have lunch. While there, he checked out women that worked in the office and made all types of comments about how good or bad certain women looked. The guys loved that he seemed so "cool" and down to earth just enough to hang out with the fellas in the cafeteria high school style.

Johnny X was a low-key guy that sat back and listened to what everyone had to say. His colleague Eric, on the other hand, would join D. Moore in the banter almost every day. So much so that it almost seemed like they were in competition to see who could point out the most attractive women for the day. Often times, Johnny X would just chuckle a little with the guys and venture off quietly on his own.

This went on for a few months until one day D. Moore stopped having lunch with the fellas. His workload had picked up and it was the normal crew back in the cafeteria without the clout of the HR Director at the table. Eric easily assumed leadership of the conversations and they were back to scoping out women.

One afternoon, Johnny X was working on a project in the main conference room, which was located next to the HR office. D. Moore walked into the room with about five other executives dressed in full suits. Johnny X had never seen them before, but they looked important. They all had serious looks on their faces. Wearing a suit with his shoulders slightly hunched over was his buddy Eric; he was walking behind this group of men. Derrick asked Johnny X to give up the conference room so that they could have their meeting in private.

It turned out that Eric had been reported for sexual harassment for overly flirting with a female manager in his division. Ironically, D. Moore had to call for the investigation and ultimately fire Eric. Eric could not understand why D. Moore didn't help to save his job after all the casual conversations that they had about women during lunch. Eric had let his guard down and fell into the trap of comfort around the boss. Johnny X always kept quiet, knowing that at any time D. Moore could switch up because after all, he is Human Resources.

The moral of this story is to never let your professional guard down. Always be "on" because at any time the rules and corporate policy can come into play. You don't have to be a stick in the mud, but never feel totally comfortable to let it all hang out at work. *Never*—regardless of the circumstances. Even if it's ten people present and nine of them are acting up. If it's an extremely inappropriate case like this one, just remove yourself from the situation altogether.

Thou shall not share new ideas with colleagues.

Picasso once said, "Good artists copy, great artists steal." Since there are a lot of people in Corporate America who practice and live by this adage, it is really important to keep your ideas close to the vest. You may have the next Facebook, create the next iPhone, or simply have the idea to launch a new program that will save your company. It's too risky to share with a co-worker who's either jealous of your current success or looking for a come up.

Please believe that more people have been stealing ideas and advancing their careers off of the backs of naïve and overly trusting colleagues since the beginning of time. Instead of fessing up to it once they are busted, some will play dumb or claim having a case of "cryptomnesia," a little-known memory glitch which involves mistaking a memory for an original thought. They will keep it moving just enough to get credit for your work.

One of the more famous instances was the invention of the telephone. Alexander Graham Bell and Elisha Gray both invented the telephone in 1876. The two inventors were racing to create a device that could transmit intelligible sounds from one place to another. On February 14, 1876, Gray submitted a patent to the United States Patent Office. On the exact same day, Bell's lawyer submitted a full patent application with a very similar diagram. There is evidence that a patent officer was bribed to give Bell the details of Gray's invention and that this formed the basis of his harmonic transmitter, which he used to send the world's first phone call. There is strong evidence that the crucial first step was supplied to him by Gray's work. Mission accomplished.

Of course, there are some appropriate moments when you should share ideas and show off your creativity. When you are working in a healthy, collaborative office environment, ideas will and should be shared and discussed openly. Brainstorming meetings where co-workers may provide the missing link you have been searching for, or build on the idea you've already started, are appropriate forums to do so. Once this idea is established as a team project, you have to make sure you're covertly marketing the fact that it was your original idea. The more ways you can publicize it, the better your chances are of getting credit for it. Furthermore, while this may seem counter-intuitive, one of the best ways to leave your handprint is to acknowledge that others have contributed to it. It's fine to mention the collaboration and give credit where it is due.

When you have new ideas outside of the scope of a brainstorming session, write them down, put them in a notebook, a word document, or even record a voice memo on your cell phone. *Never* share an idea with a co-worker one-on-one—*even* when you're hanging out with your closest colleague/confidants. You need to keep it to yourself until it's time to present them to the managers or the people who could implement them. Once you're ready to present your idea, make sure to email it in detail and cc everyone you can, including yourself. This will timestamp your idea and protect you from theft.

If you have an idea that needs a few questions answered, you need to go about it very covertly. No one should know what type of case that you are building until it's ready.

Thou shall not share career goals with peers.

Your career goals are something that you should keep near and dear to your heart. Often, your co-workers may be curious about your long-term goals to either just be in your business or to figure out if you are their competition. There is nothing worse than working with someone that you considered a friend become a competitor. Although your co-workers may appear to be happy for your success or supportive of your ambition, it's conditional. In most cases, as long as they are doing okay with progressing in their career, life is good.

However, when you both have the same aspirations and there are only so many positons to go around, you get to see their true colors. It's like when the two finalist are on stage for the Miss Universe Pageant. They are holding hands and smiling like they are sisters that have been through so much together. The reality is, one is about to be Miss Universe with a life of money, fame, speaking tours, and notoriety. The other one is about to become the woman that lost Miss Universe. Do you think that those women wouldn't directly or indirectly knock their competition to give themselves the extra edge?

Here is an example of business over friendship from an anonymous source:

As a teenager, I worked at a grocery store where I was liked by everyone. I was a buggy-boy, which is basically the person who gathers shopping carts out of the parking lot and dumps all of the trash cans in the building. I worked four days a week with my buddy Nate who was a few years older than me and had worked the lot at least two years before

I got there. We spent a lot of time together and talked about everything. I trusted him because this was my co-worker. I suffered day after day in the hot sun, hauling baskets with a bungee cord.

One day while I was working with Nate, I told him that I was tired of working outside and that I wanted to apply for a job as a cashier inside of the grocery store. He said it was a great idea. I explained to him that the only problem was that I had to be 18-years-old to work as a cashier, but that the manager was going to do me a favor and let me get trained anyway. About a month into working as a cashier and earning more money per hour, my manager told me that they had to demote me back to a buggy handler because they found out that I wasn't old enough to be a cashier. I found out that Nate went to the head store manager and ratted me out because he wanted the position as well.

I treated him like he was my friend and *not* part of the establishment. I knew he was sleeping in the storage room, but never said a word because I thought we were friends. Maybe we were to a certain degree, but he just had to shut me down to elevate himself. He had made a business decision for himself and our friendship, whether real or fake, was second to his ambitions. – Anonymous

The moral of the story is that you must be "on" at all times. Never let your guard down completely because you never know who is listening or who is willing to take you down to get ahead. Your colleagues become the competition and some will step on your neck to get ahead. Don't give them the bullets to shoot you down.

Thou shall not be transparent.

This is one of the most important lessons that you need to survive in the corporate world. Following the code that you are supposed to be "on" at all times, you should never let people see the behind-the-scenes. People have a tendency to have that one person that they are close with or team that they have become comfortable with to see them in their rawest, most uncut form. It's one of the biggest mistakes you can make.

You do not want people to learn your tricks of the trade in terms of how you go about doing things. People try to get close to you to learn your techniques to not only adopt your best practices, but to also sabotage you or use it to elevate themselves above you.

On the other hand, people may be in awe of your skills, but after seeing your approach, they may not feel you're as great as you once appeared. If someone thinks that something that you're doing is great, let them keep thinking it. It gives you power. No one ever needs to know how easy or how hard your job is.

Additionally, you don't want to share your real feelings with your co-workers. You never want to be vulnerable or show weakness, as either can be used against you at a later date. Even though sometimes it's necessary to tell an old failure story to relate to a co-worker from time to time, you should never show the hand you're holding.

This is not instruction to pretend to be something that you are not. It is not encouraged to masquerade as a subject matter expert or pretend to have more power or influence than you really have.

The Wizard in the *Wizard of Oz* had an image that was bigger than life with a loud thunderous voice, smoke and mirrors, and a reputation that had never truly been tested and proven.[15]

Just like the Wizard, being exposed as a phony person can potentially ruin your reputation forever. Everyone wants to see what's behind your curtain, especially if it proves that you're empty. Remain a mystery.

A great example of protecting your curtain is the professional football team based in Boston, MA. These 6-time champions are masterful at keeping their issues secret from the media and the general public. Their QB hid injuries and team issues so that other teams could not take that information and exploit it. Back in 2018, the QB suffered a deep cut on his throwing hand that he thought would end his season. Instead of letting people know when it happened, he kept it a secret for as long as he could. His hand was stitched, but not shown to many people. He even wore a glove on his hand while speaking to the media throughout the playoffs. He went on to defeat Jacksonville in the Conference Championship. They didn't have enough time to process the thumb that was severely compromised. Throughout his career he has been consistent about not showing people all of his behind-the-scenes ingredients to success. Even his so-called behind-the-scenes documentaries are heavily calculated.

Do not let anyone into your personal life issues, health issues, or relationship drama. Sometimes in moments of empathy and vulnerability, people share deep secrets about themselves to others to show that they are relatable or that they share the person's suffering. Do not do this. Today's ailing person is tomorrow's competition for a new role.

It's like running for office when dealing with a competitor or a hater; when election time rolls around, their skeletons and short comings are fair game. Politicians will cover for each other for the most heinous and hypocritical actions, but will rip each other to shreds in a primary. Instead, use the old parable way of conveying a point. Tell stories without indicting yourself.

Thou shall listen.

Complaining about the job or people *at* the job is a common pastime in the office, and it's a great time to gather the latest intelligence on anything and everyone.

What you have to understand is that complaining is an emotional response to hurt feelings and pressure. People often cut loose and forget about their surroundings once they are venting about their problem. More importantly, they look for like-minded people who agree with their position on a given topic. Some of the best information will be given to you from a person who's upset. The "unlock code" to the ugly truth is raw emotions. I know people may say they are against gossiping or that they hate listening to complaining co-workers, but you have to remember that this is an exercise in intelligence gathering. Why is it important to listen? It's free intel; you get to learn about people around you, and you learn about your colleagues' motives.

Listening to complainers gives you all the juicy information on a silver platter without requiring anything in return. You will learn who their friends and enemies are, what ticks them off, and what their future plans are as a result of this information.

Since the people you talk to each day in the office may show you their representative, having someone else venting about them gives you an inside track on people you may not fully know. Be careful though. You cannot always believe everything you hear. Some things will require more research, or at the least, another co-signer to vouch for the information.

If you know what people are angry about, you will start to understand why people act and move the way they do. When people are scratching their heads to understand why someone made a certain decision, you will be two steps ahead of the game because you will already know.

Being a complainer is not recommended. You do not want to be the employee in the office that no one wants to talk to because you're always minutes away from a long rant about something that happened to you. In other words, you don't want to be labeled as the perpetual victim in everyone's eyes. Victims are not leaders; instead, they are nuisances that suck the energy out of the room. Victims are seen as weak, which is a definite attack on your character. You don't want to be the one giving out intel because complainers talk a lot, and they often provide a considerable amount of important information while creating a lane of sympathy for themselves.

Should you complain, it may get back to the person you're complaining about. In an effort to maintain your poker face, you can never talk bad about your co-workers because it will definitely get back to that person. The damage could be irreparable.

Finally, you don't want to look like a snake. Believe it or not, there are still some goodie-two-shoes out there and you could ruin your brand forever if they view you as a snake. They will be afraid to open up to you because they will think that you're not trustworthy to hold their secrets.

Even though you now know you shouldn't be a complainer, you need to understand how to handle the ones around you. There are certain things you must do to keep them talking to you. First, you always need to listen intently and give off good body language. Secondly, respond to the emotion of the person, not to the insults towards people they are talking about. When a person is venting about a problem they are having, this is an emotional response. As they are talking, it's always good to acknowledge their feelings when they are upset. The easiest responses are the ones that appeal to the speaker and make them feel like they have a right to feel the way they feel about a situation, even when they're wrong.

Johnny X worked with a young lady named Mary at a call center. She often vented to him on their lunch break about their manager who was always riding them about needing to take more calls per hour. She complained that she was picked on personally because the manager was jealous of her. Johnny X often got sick of hearing about this green-eyed manager that Mary swore was hating on her every day. However, Johnny X realized that in between the venting, she talked about the special committee that she was on and explained all the new activities and changes that were coming down the pike. Mary talked about the other managers and employees as well. She'd spill the beans about things she would never mention if she wasn't angry. Each day, Johnny X bought her a soda from the vending machine, and ask her with a chuckle, "So what's going on in the neighborhood today?" That's the only opening that she would need.

Mary would go off for the entire break. Johnny X would respond with only vanilla comments just to keep her going. This reassured her that she had the green light to continue.

In contrast, Johnny X learned his lesson about just being a good listener with one of his other co-workers when she was venting about her work schedule. His former team member Kelly often complained about having to work every Saturday, while the manager always skipped out early. Johnny X explained to her how many times she was late during the week when she was in college and that the manager was right to schedule her on Saturdays. Needless to say, Kelly didn't want to hear it. She just wanted to vent and have him listen. Not be checked. After that conversation, she cut Johnny X off from communications and all the intelligence he could have been receiving. To make matters worse, Kelly was eventually promoted to a supervisor position and she was no longer interested in having conversations with Johnny X about her problems because she said that he was too judgmental. Again, lesson learned.

The third way to handle a complainer when asked a specific question about dealing with disputes with another person, is to always recommend that they talk to the person one-on-one. You can add that it's what you would do. Do not take sides. Do not pile on more dirt that you know about the other person. You can also acknowledge that the situation is messed up without blaming the other individual. For example, you can respond with, "That's a tough situation."

Thou shall not date a colleague.

This is not a dating manual or a book about dating, but we have to touch on this topic. In light of all the recent scandals and movements launching all over social media about sexual harassment and assaults that have happened in the workplace, I just encourage people to consider the risks when choosing to get involved with a co-worker. Some will counter this argument with the fact that certain individuals have successfully maintained office romances and even found spouses as a result. However, the odds of that happening most of the time are like the odds of a 5'7" point guard getting drafted to play professional basketball. It's surely possible, but not likely.

With social media being a prevalent platform, it's easier to interact with colleagues under the auspices of it being considered your "free" time, but Tweets and Facebook posts are often used to make cases against people who are accused of deviant behavior.

Often these relationships start in secrecy with strict ground rules and consideration of the co-workers that could be impacted. Eventually, someone figures out that your lunch buddy is more than just a friend, and now everything you do is judged against the fact that you're involved with a co-worker. Accusations of jealousy, favoritism, and cloudy judgement become part of your professional reputation. It takes you down a notch professionally in the eyes of senior management. You're less likely to be considered for senior level positions because the company doesn't want a potential sex scandal on their hands.

The movie *Disclosure* with Michael Douglas and Demi Moore is a great example of sexual harassment in the workplace. Bob Garvin (Michael Douglas) was a technology company founder that planned to retire when his company merged with a larger company. Instead, Meredith Johnson, a former girlfriend of Bob's, was promoted within his company to be his boss. He hung out in the office with her after hours having a bottle of wine and things got very interesting. She forced herself on him and when he turned her down, she filed a sexual harassment claim against him and drama ensued.[16]

Sex scandals are one of the most humiliating experiences to recover from professionally, and depending on what industry you are in, they can follow you forever.

All workplace environments are vulnerable to office romances. Film sets are notorious for them. Numerous productions involved the cast and/ or the crew having these sort of relationships. For example, Angelina Jolie and Brad Pitt starred in a great film called *Mr. & Mrs. Smith*.[17]

Brad and Angelina fell in love on the set, got married, and the whole nine. But look at how they ended up. When the news of their steamy romance first erupted, they were in the tabloids every week with intimate details of their personal lives exposed to the public for scrutiny and ridicule. It's safe to say that they both suffered professionally as a result of it. Fortunately, they both were rich and still moderately famous enough to move on, but "Tyrone Jenkins" and "Becky Johnson" who work for Acme Rental cars may not make it out of a bad office breakup so easily.

Although people have sometimes found their spouses in the office, we are going to focus on a few brief and obvious perils of dating at work. In a lot of cases, people are having to choose between risking their blossoming career for a new flame, or falling from grace as a result of a failed love affair.

One of the worse consequences that could happen in these situations is to have the relationship turn sour. You are now in a hostile working environment with someone you've been intimate with. The sexual harassment and ethics laws all apply, and you can now be terminated from your job. Some of the residual effects are the negative impact that your professional reputation could have in your industry. It could lead to closed doors in your face. You don't want to wear the scarlet letter at work for being known as either a slimy womanizer or the woman who slept her way to the top. Although these labels can be unfairly given and altogether rude, it happens. These labels are very difficult to shake.

In the movie *Boomerang*, the main character Marcus Graham was a talented marketing manager that started dating his colleague and boss Jacqueline Broyer. They had a very romantic relationship that ended with her just wanting to be friends. Marcus was so depressed, his work began to suffer. Not learning his lesson, he started dating a second woman in his department named Angela. She helped him out of his depression and resurrected his career. He then cheated on Angela, she broke his heart, and he was forced to quit his job.

Again, this is not an office dating manual, but only some high level advice on how to avoid a potentially devastating pitfall within your career. Office dating is a big risk with serious ramifications. It's strongly encouraged that if you are serious about reducing risks, to give it some serious consideration before you venture down that road. Your career can be over before it even starts. *If* you have already experienced a set-back due to dating in the workplace, learn from it, make peace with the person you were in the relationship with for closure, and move on.

Thou shall have a Plan B, C, and D.

It's often said that you need to have a back-up plan to your master plan because you never know what can happen in any given situation. However, in today's digital world of social media and 24-hour news cycles, you need to have a back-up plan to the back-up plan, to back up the back-up plan.

Some will tell you that having a Plan B proves that you don't believe in your Plan A. That's not true. Having an adjustment to your core plan only means that your plan is robust and has variables built into it in case of set-backs or emergencies.

Whether it's because the variables change or resources that you thought you had are no longer available, you have to be flexible enough to adjust to any situation. Senior managers appreciate an employee's ability to execute tasks on the fly. The cool thing about it is that it's not necessarily on the fly; people are not able to see behind your curtain to know that you have created contingency plans to make sure you complete your project.

Furthermore, having a back-up plan saves you from sabotage. In those cases where someone is trying to set you up by deleting your presentation "by accident" or giving you incorrect data, having Plan B to get your information right is paramount.

Johnny X worked for a technology company in 2016 and he was invited to an all-team meeting at his company headquarters in Dallas, TX. This was the first time that the entire company was meeting together in person to review all of the programs that they were working on for the current fiscal year. Johnny X took over one of the largest communications programs and was going to have to do a 30-minute presentation on it in front of the new Senior Vice-President Megan Jones who was taking over the division.

Johnny X thought this would be a good time to make a good impression because Megan hadn't worked with him before and it was rumored that she was looking to promote a few people to her senior staff. Everyone in their department knew this and some people felt like they should be considered over others based on their seniority or with whom they were already working. New-comers like Johnny X were frowned upon by the tenured brass who were afraid of his talent and abilities.

Johnny X worked on his presentation for days at a time, but he needed some additional data from his colleague Jen from whom he had taken over the contract. She was reluctant to give it to him because she thought he was going to shine like a rock star and potentially take away her opportunity to be promoted. When he approached her, she only gave him data from the last six months, claiming that it was the only metrics that she had. She told him that Megan would only want the last six months and that she wouldn't be interested in his future plans and ideas. After all, she hadn't planned on covering any new or future plans for her program and she definitely didn't want him to do it.

Johnny X was a smart guy, and he experienced a few instances of subtle sabotage from Jen already, so he decided that he needed to make sure that he was fully prepared for anything. This would be a first impression that could affect his career for years to come. He reached out to the owner of the SharePoint site. He pulled all the folders that contained metrics for the entire fiscal year. He met with a few project managers to put together a plan for the upcoming fiscal year, but he saved it on a thumb drive and made another copy of his presentation that he had to present to Megan.

When they got to the meeting, Johnny X and Jen were very cordial with each other. The meeting started off very tense, as Jen's Manager was really unorganized and she had made many missteps early in the morning that made her look very inept as a manager. The conference room that was supposed to be reserved for the day had not been locked down, so the team, along with the Vice President as well as all the snacks, had to be moved to another room that wasn't as comfortable as the original.

After they moved and started to get settled in their new chairs, the large conference room became available and everyone elected to move back into the main conference room. It was the only room that had a working audio center to run the Power Point presentations. Once they were set up, Jen furnished her presentation and it went through with a few hiccups, but for the most part, it was okay. She fumbled through a few of the confusing slides that contained too much text, but the worst part was when she could not answer any of the questions the VP had. Megan was very smart, and she wouldn't let Jen get away with finessing her way through a few points she apparently did not know.

When it was Johnny X's turn to present, the VP was visibly unimpressed with what she had travelled from her San Francisco office to see. He recognized the bad energy and didn't want it to affect the response to his presentation, so he pushed for the team to take their 20-minute break at that moment.

Once everyone returned, Johnny X felt the energy come back to the room. Everyone had used the restroom, replenished their coffee cups and snack plates, and was ready to work again. He presented and it went through smoothly without any errors. Megan was actually quite impressed with his Power Point abilities and presentation skills. He was very creative in how his information was structured and he realized that Megan was impressed. Jen had noticed too, so when he asked if they had any questions, Megan asked if she could hear more about what their plans were for the next fiscal year.

The Manager politely interrupted Megan to say they weren't ready to discuss it yet because they were waiting for direction and a new budget from her. Johnny X noticed a troubled look on Megan's face. Megan looked at the Manager like she hit her on the back of her ankles with a shopping cart. Jen tried to seize this moment to get some shine over her Manager and Johnny X. She flipped through her notebook to a scribbled page with prepared notes to share her thoughts on the program. Megan seemed unimpressed, and once again asked if they had a plan to present.

After watching his Manager and Jen die a slow and agonizing death, Johnny X raised his hand. "Yes Megan. I have FY16 year plan for you to review. I put a plan together to give you a better view of how I envision improving all of our programs while saving us money and maintaining our current headcount," he responded confidently.

Megan sat up in her chair with intrigue as if Johnny X offered her a cocktail. Jen and the Manager looked on like the evil step-sisters from Cinderella waiting for her to try on the glass slipper. Johnny X removed the thumb drive from around his neck and loaded up a 30-slide deck that was more glorious than the one he had just presented.

Suddenly, he and Megan appeared to be having a one-on-one meeting in the presence of his entire team. Once he finished, Megan was super excited about what she had seen and concluded not only did Johnny X provide her with some great ideas that they would surely use going forward, but she also had some immediate opportunities for him to work on.

That experience taught Johnny X to make sure that he's not only prepared, but to have multiple plans in place just in case. Preparation is the pre-season to opportunity. Like training in the off-season for the professional basketball combine with running, putting up shots, and pick-up games, your preparation will tell the story when your season (opportunity) comes around. Preparation also means that you have opportunities to fall back on when those new or unexpected challenges arise. Not only should you have contingency plans in case things go wrong, but you should anticipate what your boss or potential business partner may need. Sometimes you may create something that you don't end up using, but it will ultimately help you in the long run. You can never have too much content or too many ideas laying around.

Thou shall over-dress and then dress it down.

If you don't nail the outfit, it's always a good idea to over-dress for an event or activity when involving the workplace. It's often far easier to dress down than it is to dress up.

For men, a suit and tie can be dressed down to just a button-down with the sleeves rolled up, but jeans and a polo cannot be business casual. Keep a tie in the office.

For women, there are various ways to adjust their look to fit the appropriate moment and setting. An idea that has proven helpful is to have an extra outfit either in the office or in the car.

For both men and women, never wear sandals (ever) and always keep a blazer on hand for those emergency moments.

Thou shall protect oneself.

People will tell you that there are two types of people in the world: good people and bad people. The problem is that sometimes you can never tell who is who until it is too late. Nice people are often taken advantage of when their nature is to put everyone in the "good person" category, and then remove them once they are scorned or double-crossed in a particular moment or critical situation.

The problem with this approach is that people assume that a "snake" is a "German shepherd" and that they are loyal defenders of their brand and have a vested interest in their success. In reality, most people in Corporate America operate with their own best interest in mind first and foremost; they're snakes. If your best interests doesn't hinder them in anyway, they may appear to be allies, or a loyal defending German shepherd. What makes this a huge challenge is that it often takes a long time to figure out the real character of a person.

The approach in most people's eyes is in reverse. Instead of starting everyone in the good person category, you should start them in the bad one first. Make them earn their spot in your good people bucket, or category. Feel them out, give them opportunities to prove their loyalty, and to earn brownie points with you. This way you are not disappointed when they prove to be a terrible, selfish, or cut-throat person like you anticipated them to be.

With good people, you can collaborate with them, share small things, and build the relationship into a positive part of your network. However, even if they are good people, you still need to remember the Office Game Commandments and apply the rules. You are on at all times no matter what.

Individuals prove their worth by their willingness to help you, open doors/opportunities, and not sell you out in interactions with senior managers.

With bad people, you should not treat them any different from the good people. You just have to appreciate the fact that you have been able to identify them early on and act accordingly. You should never trust them or share things with them, so they won't have leverage against you.

What's crazy is when bad people attempt to become good again and get back in your good graces. What you need to always be mindful of is that you do not know their motives. They may need something from you or may try to take you down. Don't fall for the banana in the tail-pipe. You can agree to a truce on the surface, but remember at all times that they are the bad guy.

Thou shall be good to everyone.

One of the oldest sayings that my mother used to say was, "Never burn your bridges, because you never know when you will need to cross back."

I have always tried to live my life that way in the business world. No matter how bad a person treated me on the job, or what they said about me, I never intentionally threw anyone under the bus. This included those times when they deserved it and was asking for it.

There were times I went home wanting to punch a hole in the wall after someone tried to sabotage me at work. Throwing my co-working villains under the bus would have been sweet revenge for some of the capers that a few of these beloved colleagues tried to pull on me.

There were times when I could have sacrificed a co-worker to elevate myself. Good and bad people could have been brought to the guillotine on my behalf. Instead, due to my good nature and the sound advice from my mother, I refrained.

What time has shown me about exacting revenge on a bad person who deserves it, is that it's not worth it. It's not worth the risk of ruining my reputation and chasing people away who trust and respect me. Throwing someone under the bus backfires as well.

I have personally witnessed people attempt to throw someone under the bus by outing their methods for making their quota numbers every month to look good. Back when I was working as a cell phone vendor for a large multinational corporation, cell phone sales were not as frequent as they are in the age of the smartphone. All salesman were required to sell a certain amount of phones each week and we had to record the ESN numbers on the back of the box the phone was packaged in as proof.

We had a guy named Barry that was selling so many phones, that his production raised everyone's quota for the week. What was irritating was that every week we had a sales meeting, he won the extra commission and sales award. Barry wasn't humble about it either. He rubbed it in our faces every chance he got, told our regional manager that we weren't working as hard as he was, and that he should have the prime stores in the larger shopping malls that were more desirable locations. We hated him. The other sales people talked smack about him amongst ourselves, but that was about as far as it would go. One of the salesman named Reese was skeptical of our co-worker's success, and said that he wouldn't rest until he got to the bottom of it.

One day, Reese was sent to one of Barry's stores because ironically, he was on a vacation compliments of his most recent sales bonus. He was stationed in an electronics store called T.V. City that sold our cell phone product. He was there for about two hours when the Electronics Manager walked over to him with a spreadsheet and receipts stapled to it. "I know Barry is on vacation, but he told me that he still needs to have these," he said.

Reese was confused when he took the paperwork. "What are these?" he asked.

"These are the sales and receipts for the phones we sold all week while you all were gone," the Electronics Manager responded.

Reese realized how Barry had been making those awesome sales numbers and he couldn't wait to let Barry and the rest of us know, but not before he got paid himself. So he took the paperwork and left the store for the day.

When the numbers came out for the month, Reese's numbers were just as high as Barry's. We all were excited, but Barry was angry. For the first time in about six months, Barry was not the top dog. Everyone in the meeting was anxious to find out how Reese beat Barry out that month. I personally was happy that Barry lost for once. He was extremely salty about it.

Our Regional Manager started the meeting by congratulating everyone for their hard work for the month. She congratulated Reese individually for his accomplishment. Instead of being modest, he took this opportunity to rub it in Barry's face in front of the boss. He thought that it would be a great idea to expose Barry's sales secret. So as he was thanking the Regional Manager for her recognition, he changed gears and began explaining how Barry was beating us out every month and how he intercepted the numbers for that month from the Electronics Manager at T.V. City. We were amazed. However, when he finished, Barry's head dropped and he put both hands over his sunken face like Maury just told him that he was the father. Our Regional Manager stopped him; she stood up and asked everyone to leave the room except for Barry and Reese. We all walked out looking confused, but glad that it wasn't us that was asked to stay.

After about 15-20 minutes, Reese and Barry both walked out with their heads hanging low and neither one was wearing their company issued Polo shirt anymore. Barry walked past us wearing a dingy V-neck white T-shirt and a backwards baseball cap. He mumbled, "Reese ruined everything" under his breath and left out the front glass double doors.

They had been fired. Reese walked out second and he had a dumbfound look on his face too. "What the hell happened in there?" I asked.

Reese explained that our Regional Manager was watching Barry for about two months and realized that he was claiming commission credits for phones that he didn't even sell. He had a scheme working with the Electronics Manager. She was trying to get enough proof to fire him. Sadly, Reese had done the same undercover investigation with the goal to stick it to Barry. So now they both were out. Had he not used those numbers, he would still have his job.

In the end, Barry was going to get his anyway. Bad people doing bad things usually do themselves in when it's all said and done.

Post-Game Takeaways:

✗ Apply the 10 Office Commandments to your workplace: (1) thou shall be aware, (2) thou shall not share new ideas with colleagues, (3) thou shall not share career goals with peers, (4) thou shall not be transparent, (5) thou shall listen, (6) thou shall not date a colleague, (7) thou shall have Plan B, C, and D, (8) thou shall over-dress and dress it down, (9) thou shall protect oneself, and (10) thou shall be good to everyone.

*** GAME TIP ***

When showing someone how to do something, *never* give your full process or special procedure away. Your secret sauce is what separates your Big Mac from someone's Whopper. When helping someone out, give them the bare minimum to get started and set up their structure. Never go higher than 30% when you can manage it. If they ask for more, it may be good to have them send you the document or product so that you can finish it by yourself. Do not give out full templates, secret contacts that only you have, or software tricks that you learn outside of the office.

*** GAME TIP ***

When a person resigns from your company and provides you with their contact information, take it and call them. Not only is it a connection for the future, but they'll be ready to tell you everything they know about the company. Good or bad, it will be great to get this perspective.

Playbook Notes

CHAPTER 8

GOING FORWARD

Pre-Game Analysis:

✗ Learn what to do once you put it all together.

✗ Continue to grow and enhance your skills.

Having Office Game is not about learning how to manipulate people and cheat the system. It is about knowing what the system is, and what it's not, *only* to protect yourself from the politics, hating, and incompetence that can exist in Corporate America, while having the ability to thrive in it.

When a person says someone has game in any facet of life, they are acknowledging that they recognize a superior level of intelligence, knowledge, and wisdom pertaining to the specific subject area at hand. Having this insight in itself is not the end all be all.

For example, take relationships. A man who is viewed as a "Player" is usually construed as a person that has a great understanding of how relationships work and the nuances associated with it. They know how to successfully navigate through the traps and perils that most people fall victim to throughout their own experiences. Consequently, they are typically categorized as a person who uses their relationship acumen for evil rather than for good.

On the positive side, credit and reverence is often given to the old senior citizen sitting on the park bench imparting wisdom to the young generation that is perceived to be so self-absorbed they don't understand how life really works. Younger generations of people can sometimes be dismissive when the O.G. are giving them game. They assume that his information, although useful to a certain extent, falls short because he/she's missing how the advanced relationship lanes within the new generation don't apply to old school principles.

What people fail to realize is that the so-called dated values and ideologies are transferable philosophies that translate to new generations as well. Times change, technology increases, and people evolve, but human nature remains the same. Knowing about a certain subject area is one thing, but understanding how to successfully traverse through it is where having real game lies.

Knowing how to navigate the hurdles of corporate bureaucracy/hypocrisy and career competition starts with understanding the office environment and culture, then navigating through it using your previous experience, your ability to observe and analyze what's going on around you, and the ability to execute accordingly.

A professional basketball player can put you in a classroom and show you everything there is to know about basketball. They could even wake up with you and do a 2-hour training session every day for six months. However, until you actually go out and play in a game to showcase what you have learned, you will never know your true skill level. You don't know how it feels to get slapped on the arm while shooting a layup, until you're actually in the game playing against fierce competition while the referee is looking the other way as you get beat up on offense and called for ticky-tack fouls on defense. It's in these moments that you lean on your preparation, fundamentals, and internal fortitude to overcome your adversity to achieve victory. It's often said that experience is the best teacher, and that's true. How much more poised for victory would you be once you are in the midst of these experiences with stellar insight and comprehensive preparation backing you up?

You are ultimately in control of your career. Every experience that you have and the people that you interact with help shape you as a professional. They will either help you build yourself up to the highest heights of your potential, or help break you down to the lowest of the lows in your worst case scenario. It all comes down to how you handle adversity, both self-inflicted and/or created by others. It's how you take advantage of the opportunities presented to you by being focused, prepared, and resolute.

Learning the basics of the Office Game gives you a foundation that can carry you throughout your career. These basic principles can evolve with the industry you're working in and through personal experiences. There are best practices to adopt that will help shape your professional image and enhance your ability to connect with people. You will have meaningful and professional relationships, while overcoming the trappings of haters and career con-artists who are either trying to ride your wave or take you down. Now that you have the game, go be great!

Post-Game Takeaways:

✗ Always understand that if you're part of Corporate America, you're in the game whether you actively choose to play or not. The game will find you.

✗ Always remember that you have to be on at all times, so avoid letting your guard down.

✗ Apply the tools provided within this book, continue to learn, grow, and be successful.

> ### *** GAME TIP ***
>
> Always be on, know how and when to play, and be the best professional version of yourself.

Playbook Notes

_____
_____
_____
_____
_____
_____
_____
_____
_____
_____
_____
_____
_____
_____
_____
_____
_____
_____

About the Author

With over 20 years of Corporate America experience in multiple industries and the owner and president of Kossen Communications LLC, K.V. Scott is a seasoned veteran in the world of business professionals.

For nearly a decade, K.V.'s own consulting company has been providing internal communications and marketing expertise to small businesses, U.S. government agencies, and large multinational corporations.

This University of New Orleans graduate continues to thrive and succeed both as a consultant and as a senior communications manager for a large global technology corporation.

Notes

1   *Pretty Woman.* Gary Marshall. Touchstone Pictures, 1990.

2   *Fast and the Furious.* Rob Cohen. Universal Pictures, 2001.

3   *Boomerang.* Reginald Hudlin. Paramount Pictures and Imagine Films Entertainment, 1992.

4   *Malcolm X.* Spike Lee. Largo International, N.V., 1992.

5   *John Q.* Nick Cassavetes. New Line Cinema, 2002.

6   *Mo' Money.* Peter MacDonald. Columbia Pictures Corporation, 1992.

7   Greene, Robert. *The 48 Laws of Power.* United States: Viking Penguin, 2000.

8   *Bad Boys.* Michael Bay. Don Simpson/Jerry Bruckheimer Films, 1995.

9   *New Jack City.* Mario Van Peebles. Warner Brothers, 1991.

10 *The Matrix.* Lana Wachowski and Lilly Wachowski. Warner Brothers, 1999.

11 O'Jays. "Back Stabbers." *Back Stabbers,* Legacy/Epic Associated, 1972. CD.

12 *A League of their Own.* Penny Marshall. Columbia Pictures Corporation, 1992.

13 Jay-Z. "Takeover." *The Blueprint,* Roc A Fella, 2001. CD.

14 Patti Labelle. "New Attitude." *Live! One Night Only,* MCA, 1998. CD.

15 Wizard of Oz. Victor Fleming. Metro-Goldwyn-Mayer, 1939.

16 Disclosure. Barry Levinson. Warner Brothers, 1994.

17 Mr. & Mrs. Smith. Doug Liman. Regency Enterprises, 2005.

Made in the USA
Monee, IL
21 January 2021